THE KITCHEN LIBRARY

ITALIAN COOKING

D0313483

ITALIAN COOKING

Mary Reynolds

OCTOPUS BOOKS

CONTENTS

NOTES
Standard spoon measurements are used in all recipes
1 tablespoon = one 15 ml spoon
1 teaspoon = one 5 ml spoon
All spoon measures are level.

Fresh herbs are used unless otherwise stated. If
unobtainable substitute a bouquet garni of the
equivalent dried herbs, or use dried herbs
instead but halve the quantities stated.

Use freshly ground black pepper where pepper
is specified.

Ovens should be preheated to the specified temperature.

For all recipes, quantities are given in both metric
and imperial measures. Follow either set but not a
mixture of both, because they are not interchangeable.

This edition published 1988 by
Octopus Books Limited
Michelin House
81 Fulham Road
London SW3 6RB
Reprinted 1988
© Cathay Books 1981
ISBN 0 7064 3249 5
Printed by Mandarin Offset in Hong Kong

INTRODUCTION

The best cooking in Italy is found in the home. Italian women take a special pleasure in shopping for the best quality ingredients and in cooking attractive meals for their families.

The main meal of the day is an important event; a social occasion when all the family gather around the table to exchange the news and gossip of the day and to share in the enjoyment of mama's cooking. A traditional Italian meal – although infinitely flexible – generally consists of a minestra (soup, pasta dish, or risotto), followed by a course of meat, fish or poultry with one or two vegetables. Sometimes a raw salad vegetable is served afterwards. The meal ends with cheese and fresh fruit in season, and is rounded off with a small cup of strong expresso coffee. On special occasions a simple antipasto may be served before the minestra and a dessert before the fruit and cheese.

Generally speaking, hard and fast rules have no place in the Italian kitchen, so use the recipes in this book as guidelines; always testing, trying and adapting as you go along.

Italian Regional Cooking

Until 1861 Italy was a collection of independent states, each with its own laws, customs and traditions. Today, as you travel from one area to another, you will notice regional differences between the landscape, people, dialects and foods.

There is a particularly marked difference between northern and southern Italy: regions in the north tend to be more industrial and prosperous than those in the poorer south and the northern soil tends to be more fertile. The differences as far as cooking is concerned are that the traditional northern pasta is the flat variety, freshly made with eggs; the fat used for cooking is generally butter. In the south, tubular varieties of pasta are more common and olive oil is used for cooking. Flavours are much stronger in the south because of the extensive use of herbs and aromatics, particularly in sauces.

Well-known pasta dishes of the northern province of Liguria include ravioli and minestrone soup. The rice-growing area in the Po Valley, just behind Venice, provides abundant supplies of arboreo rice. This especially absorbent medium-grained rice is the basis for risottos and an excellent way of making small amounts of meat or shellfish stretch to feed a large family. Many delicious, creamy risotto recipes have evolved; risotto Milanese from Lombardy must be one of the best known.

Two of the most famous products of the north are Parmesan cheese and prosciutto ham, both from Parma. Parmesan cheese is at its best after 2 years of drying and maturing, and becomes stronger the longer it is left. The whey from the cheese is fed to the Parma pigs and, combined with the careful salting and drying processes on the hillsides, results in the delicately flavoured ham.

Italy is virtually surrounded by sea and locally caught fish are a dominant feature of most regional cuisines. Venice is particularly noted for its red and grey mullet, squid, scampi and mussels. In the north, seafish supplies are supplemented by excellent freshwater fish from the Lakes of Lombardy – especially eels. The southern coast and the islands of Sicily and Sardinia are dotted with fishing villages. Here, tuna, sardines, swordfish and a variety of shellfish are caught and used locally in pasta dishes, sauces, soups, stews and salads.

Abundant local supplies of tomatoes, garlic, herbs and anchovies in the southern regions give dishes their characteristic aromatic quality. Naples, the culinary centre of the south, claims the invention of the pizza and ice cream as we know it today. Pizzas are baked in open-brick

ovens of pizzerias and bakeries, and most often eaten as
snacks. Mozzarella, the cheese used for pizza toppings, has
been made for centuries in the surrounding countryside of
Campania. It is an ideal 'melting' cheese and lends itself to
all types of pizzas and cooked dishes. The equally famous
Italian ices are made in mouth-watering flavours and, like
the pizza, have spread all over Italy and further afield.

Italy is the world's largest wine producer and almost
every region makes its contribution to the great variety of
exported table wines. Piemonte is the home of Barolo, a
fine red to accompany roast meat and game, and the
modest but flavoursome Barbera, an ideal wine to drink
with robust pasta dishes and pizzas. Veneto provides two
popular wines: the dry, red Valpolicella and Soave – a
medium white wine. From Tuscany comes the deservedly
famous Chianti Classico, the perfect accompaniment to
roasts, grills and game dishes. Other Italian wines worth
trying are Orvieto, Verdicchio, Frascati and Lambrusco.

Specialist Italian Ingredients

Delicatessens and good supermarkets offer an ever-increasing number of Italian ingredients. Most items can be obtained from these or a simple substitute can be used.

CHEESES

Parmesan: Unique cheese, grated and added to sauces, pasta, rice and other dishes to give an incomparable flavour. It is best bought by the piece; packets of ready-grated Parmesan cannot compare with the freshly grated cheese.

Mozzarella: A white cheese, used extensively in cooking for its melting properties, especially as a topping for pizzas. It is sold in small packets and, when very fresh, is moist and dripping with whey. Bel Paese can be used as a substitute.

Ricotta: A soft, white cheese, made from whey. Must be eaten absolutely fresh. Used in savoury stuffings and sweet fillings. Low-fat curd cheese makes a good substitute.

Gorgonzola: The famous Italian blue-veined table cheese. When ripe, it should be mild and soft.

Other Italian table cheeses to look out for are Bel Paese, Pecorino, Fontina, Provolone and Caciocavallo.

CURED MEATS AND SAUSAGES

Bresaola: Dry cured beef fillet, eaten raw in wafer thin slices. A highly esteemed antipasto.

Prosciutto: Delicately cured ham, eaten raw and wafer thin. The best comes from Parma or San Daniele. No real substitute, but for cooked dishes use smoked ham.

Salami: Long dry-cured sausages of lean ground meat with pork fat and spices. There are various types, of which Salami Milano is considered the best. Serve sliced in mixed antipasti, chopped in stuffings.

Mortadella: Large smooth-textured cooked pork sausage laced with pork fat and spices. Serve sliced for antipasti, chopped in stuffings.

Cotechino: Lightly cured pork sausage, weighing from 500g to 1 kg (1 to 2 lb). It is first boiled, then thickly sliced and served with lentils or beans, or cold with salad.

Luganega: Long, thin coiled sausage of mild, coarsely ground pork. Also called *Salsiccia*. Fry, grill or boil and serve hot with lentils or potatoes. Any fresh sausage with a high meat content can be used as a substitute.

HERBS

Herbs are an essential flavouring in many Italian dishes. Fresh herbs are normally used in Italy; fortunately these are becoming increasingly available in shops. However, it is well worth growing a selection of herbs in pots on the window or in the garden. Use dried herbs when fresh ones are unavailable, but replace regularly to avoid staleness. The following are most commonly used in Italian cooking.

Basil: The incomparable herb for tomato dishes. Also popular in salads, sauces and soups.

Bay Leaves: As a flavouring for casseroles, soups and roasts; also put onto the fire at outdoor barbecues for aroma.

Oregano: Common ingredient in many dishes, especially pizzas, casseroles and sauces.

Parsley: The universal herb for flavouring Italian savoury dishes. Italian parsley is the flat-leaved variety so use this when available.

Rosemary: Strongly-flavoured herb, used mainly for roast lamb or pork. Also chicken and fish dishes.

Sage: Especially for flavouring veal and chicken dishes cooked in wine.

STORECUPBOARD INGREDIENTS

The following non-perishable ingredients are frequently used in Italian dishes and it is useful to keep a stock of them in your storecupboard.

Pasta: Available in an immense variety of shapes and used in many different ways: both the shaped pastas of the south (macaroni, spaghetti, zita, bucatini, rigatoni, etc) and the lighter, flat egg pastas of the north (tagliatelle, fettucine, lasagne, etc) are available dried in packets. Keep a range of pasta in stock – including a few of the less common shapes and small varieties for soups.

Rice: Italian arboreo rice is thicker, shorter and absorbs more liquid than other types of rice. It is essential for a creamy risotto. Italian rice is sold in an "easy cook" form.

Beans: Dried haricot beans and lentils, canned white cannelli and red borlotti beans are used for soups, salads and other dishes.

Pepper and Salt: Italians always use freshly ground black peppercorns from a pepper mill and, when possible, coarse sea salt.

Wine Vinegar: Essential for salad dressings and used in many other recipes.

Olive and Vegetable Oils: The distinctive flavour of good olive oil is needed for salad dressings and for cooking where olive oil gives the dish a special character. Otherwise ground nut or sunflower oil are suitable.

Anchovy Fillets in oil: For adding zest to sauces, pizzas and antipasti dishes.

Capers: Small capers add authenticity to various sauces, fish dishes and garnishes.

Olives: Keep small bottles or plastic packs of green, black and stuffed olives, but buy fresh loose ones when possible.

Canned Peeled Tomatoes: These Italian 'plum' tomatoes have an excellent flavour and are time-saving and convenient for all sauces and casseroles. Use them for cooking in preference to fresh English tomatoes.

Tomato Purée: Small amounts are invaluable for strengthening the flavour and colour of dishes in which fresh or canned tomatoes are used.

Fortified Wines: Dry white Vermouth can be used in recipes needing white wine and herbs; it is stronger than table wine so less is needed. Medium Marsala gives a richness to veal, poultry and ham dishes.

SAUCES

Salsa di Fegatini
Chicken Liver Sauce

50 g (2 oz) butter
1 small onion,
  chopped
50 g (2 oz)
  unsmoked streaky
  bacon, derinded
  and diced
50 g (2 oz)
  mushrooms, finely
  chopped
250 g (8 oz) chicken
  livers, diced
1 tablespoon plain
  flour
2 tablespoons
  Marsala
300 ml (½ pint)
  chicken stock
1 tablespoon tomato
  purée
salt and pepper

Melt 40 g (1½ oz) of the butter in a saucepan, add the onion and bacon and cook gently for 6 to 8 minutes, stirring occasionally. Increase the heat and add the mushrooms and chicken livers; cook, stirring, for 2 minutes. Add the flour and cook, stirring, for 1 minute.

Add the Marsala, bring to the boil, then stir in the stock, tomato purée and a little salt and pepper. Bring to the boil, cover and simmer for 30 to 40 minutes. Stir in the remaining butter and check the seasoning.

Serve hot with pasta, *Gnocchi di patate* (see page 76) or *Risotto alla paesana* (see page 29).
Serves 4

Salsa di Carne
Meat Sauce

15 g (½ oz) butter
50 g (2 oz) smoked
    streaky bacon,
    derinded and diced
1 onion, chopped
1 small carrot, diced
1 celery stick, diced
350 g (12 oz)
    minced beef
2 tablespoons plain
    flour
450 ml (¾ pint) beef
    stock
1 tablespoon tomato
    purée
salt and pepper
grated nutmeg

Melt the butter in a pan, add the bacon, onion, carrot and celery and fry gently for 10 minutes, stirring frequently. Add the beef and cook, stirring, until browned. Stir in the flour and cook for 2 minutes.

Stir in the stock and tomato purée, and season with salt, pepper and nutmeg to taste. Bring to the boil, cover and simmer for 1 hour, stirring occasionally.

Serve with pasta.

Serves 4 to 6

Ragù Bolognese
Rich Meat Sauce

15 g (½ oz) butter
50 g (2 oz) smoked
  streaky bacon,
  derinded and diced
1 onion, finely
  chopped
1 small carrot, diced
1 celery stick, diced
350 g (12 oz) finely
  minced beef
125 g (4 oz) chicken
  livers, finely
  chopped
4 tablespoons dry
  vermouth or white
  wine
300 ml (½ pint) beef
  stock
1 tablespoon tomato
  purée
salt and pepper
grated nutmeg
2 tablespoons single
  cream or top of the
  milk

Melt the butter in a saucepan, add the bacon, onion, carrot and celery and fry gently for 10 minutes, stirring frequently. Add the beef and cook, stirring, until browned. Stir in the chicken livers and vermouth or wine. Bring to the boil and cook until the liquid has almost completely evaporated.

Stir in the stock and tomato purée, and season with salt, pepper and nutmeg to taste. Bring back to the boil, cover and simmer for 1 hour, stirring occasionally. Check the seasoning and stir in the cream or milk.

Serve with tagliatelli, spaghetti or other pasta.

Serves 4 to 6

Salsa di Pomodori
Tomato Sauce (using canned tomatoes)

1 × 397 g (14 oz)
  can peeled tomatoes
1 onion, chopped
1 clove garlic, crushed
1 carrot, sliced
1 celery stick, sliced
2 teaspoons tomato
  purée
1 teaspoon sugar
salt and pepper
2 teaspoons chopped
  basil (optional)

Put the tomatoes with their juice, the onion, garlic, carrot, celery, tomato purée and sugar into a saucepan. Add a little salt and pepper and stir with a wooden spoon to break up the tomatoes. Bring to the boil, partially cover and simmer for 30 minutes.

Rub through a sieve and return to the pan. If necessary, boil rapidly, uncovered, until reduced to a sauce consistency. Check the seasoning and stir in the basil, if using.

Serve as required, with pasta or meat dishes.

Makes about 300 ml (½ pint)

Salsa Pizzaiola
Fresh Tomato and Herb Sauce

2 tablespoons olive oil
2 cloves garlic,
    crushed
625 g (1¼ lb) ripe
    tomatoes, skinned
    and chopped
1 teaspoon sugar
salt and pepper
1 tablespoon chopped
    basil, oregano or
    parsley

Heat the oil and garlic gently in a saucepan for 2 minutes. Add the tomatoes, sugar, and salt and pepper to taste. Cook briskly for a few minutes until most of the liquid has evaporated and the tomatoes have softened but not reduced to a pulp.

Use as required with steaks, chops or fish. Garnish with herbs to serve.
Serves 4

Besciamella
Béchamel Sauce

40 g (1½ oz) butter
40 g (1½ oz) plain flour
600 ml (1 pint) hot milk
salt and pepper
grated nutmeg

Melt the butter in a saucepan, add the flour and cook, stirring, for 1 minute. Remove from the heat and gradually stir in the milk.

Return to the heat and cook, stirring, until thickened. Simmer for 3 minutes. Season with salt, pepper and nutmeg to taste.

Makes about 600 ml (1 pint)
NOTE: For additional flavour, add a bay leaf to the milk before heating. Remove before adding the milk to the sauce.

Maionese

2 large egg yolks
1 teaspoon salt
2-3 teaspoons lemon juice
200 ml (⅓ pint) olive oil

Have all the ingredients at room temperature.

Put the egg yolks into a small basin, add the salt and 1 teaspoon of the lemon juice and mix thoroughly. Add the oil drop by drop, stirring constantly, until the sauce becomes thick and shiny. Add the rest of the oil in a thin stream, stirring constantly. Add lemon juice to taste.

Makes about 300 ml (½ pint)

Maionese Tonnata
Tuna Fish Mayonnaise

200 ml (⅓ pint)
   Maionese (see
   opposite)
1 × 99 g (3½ oz)
   can tuna fish
3 anchovy fillets
1 tablespoon lemon
   juice

Put the *Maionese* into an electric blender, add the remaining ingredients and work until smooth. If necessary, thin to a coating consistency by adding a little cold water.

   Alternatively, rub the undrained tuna fish and the anchovies through a sieve into a bowl. Add the egg yolks and proceed as for *Maionese* (see opposite).

   Use to coat hard-boiled eggs, sliced cold chicken, turkey or veal, or to stuff tomatoes.
Makes about 300 ml (½ pint)

Salsa Verde
Piquant Green Sauce

2 shallots
1 clove garlic
1 pickled gherkin
1 tablespoon capers
40 g (1½ oz)
   parsley
2 tablespoons lemon
   juice
6 tablespoons olive
   oil
salt and pepper

Put all the ingredients in an electric blender and work until smooth, seasoning with salt and pepper to taste.

   Alternatively, chop the first 5 ingredients together very finely. Stir in the lemon juice and oil, and season with salt and pepper to taste.

   Serve with hot or cold boiled meat, fish or poultry.
Makes about 200 ml (⅓ pint)

Stracciatella
'Ragged' Egg Soup

2 eggs
2 tablespoons fine
   semolina
50 g (2 oz) grated
   Parmesan cheese
1.2 litres (2 pints)
   Brodo di Pollo
   (see opposite)

Beat together the eggs, semolina, cheese and about 200 ml (⅓ pint) *Brodo di pollo*. Heat the remaining broth until almost boiling, immediately remove from the heat and beat in the egg mixture.

Continue beating over a low heat for 2 to 3 minutes, just until the eggs break into 'ragged' flakes. Serve immediately.

Serves 4 to 6

Brodo di Pollo
Chicken Broth

This forms the basis of many soups. The chicken can be served hot for the main course, or cold with *Salsa verde* or *Maionese tonnata* (see page 17).

1 × 1.5 kg (3 lb) oven-ready chicken
1.2 litres (2 pints) water
1 carrot, sliced
1 onion, sliced
2 celery sticks, sliced
2 tomatoes, quartered
1 bay leaf
6 peppercorns
1 teaspoon salt
1 chicken stock cube (optional)

Put the prepared chicken and giblets (except the liver) into a deep pan and add the water. Bring slowly to the boil and remove any scum. Add the vegetables, bay leaf, peppercorns and salt. Cover and simmer very gently until the chicken is tender, about 1 hour. Lift out the chicken. Strain the broth and check the seasoning; if necessary, crumble in the stock cube and stir until dissolved.

Makes about 1.2 litres (2 pints)

Passatelli in Brodo
Cheese Noodles in Broth

1.2 litres (2 pints)
  Brodo di Pollo
  (see page 19)
1 small egg, beaten
2 teaspoons flour
25 g (1 oz) grated
  Parmesan cheese
25 g (1 oz) dry
  white breadcrumbs
15 g (½ oz) butter,
  softened
pepper
grated nutmeg

Bring the *Brodo di pollo* to the boil in a large pan.

Place the egg, flour, cheese, breadcrumbs and butter in a basin. Add pepper and nutmeg to taste and work to a firm paste.

Press through a metal colander directly into the boiling broth. Simmer until the noodles rise to the surface, about 2 minutes.

Pour into individual soup bowls and serve immediately, with extra Parmesan cheese.

Serves 4 to 6

Zuppa di Zucchini
Courgette Soup

40 g (1½ oz) butter
1 onion, sliced
500 g (1 lb)
  courgettes, thinly
  sliced
1.2 litres (2 pints)
  water
1½ chicken stock
  cubes
2 small eggs
2 tablespoons grated
  Parmesan cheese
1 tablespoon chopped
  basil or parsley
salt and pepper
TO GARNISH:
crostini (see below)
  or croûtons

Melt the butter in a saucepan, add the onion and fry gently for 5 minutes. Add the courgettes and fry, stirring frequently, for 5 to 10 minutes. Add the water and stock cubes, bring to the boil, cover and simmer for 20 minutes.

Purée in an electric blender or rub through a sieve. Return to the saucepan and bring to the boil.

Beat the eggs, cheese and herbs together in a warmed soup tureen, then slowly beat in the boiling soup. Check the seasoning, and pour into individual soup bowls. Top with *crostini* or croûtons and serve immediately.

Serves 4 to 6

CROSTINI: Cut round bread rolls into 5 mm (¼ inch) thick slices and toast one side. Spread the untoasted side with butter, sprinkle thickly with grated cheese and place under a preheated hot grill until golden and bubbling.

Minestra di Frittata
Omelet Soup

1.2 litres (2 pints)
  Brodo di Pollo
  (see page 19)
2 eggs
1 tablespoon flour
4 tablespoons milk
salt and pepper
25 g (1 oz) grated
  Parmesan cheese
chopped parsley to
  garnish

Bring the *Brodo di pollo* to the boil in a large pan.

Beat the eggs with the flour, milk and a little salt and pepper.

Lightly oil a large frying pan and place over high heat. When very hot, pour in the batter and cook for about 1 minute until set. Turn out, roll up and cut into thin strips. Add to the boiling broth with the cheese.

Serve immediately, sprinkled with parsley.
Serves 4 to 6

Minestrone
Thick Vegetable Soup

175 g (6 oz) cabbage
1 large onion
1 large carrot
2 celery sticks
2 courgettes
3 tomatoes, skinned
50 g (2 oz) streaky
  bacon, derinded
2 tablespoons oil
2 cloves garlic,
  crushed
1.75 litres (3 pints)
  water
4 sage or basil
  leaves, chopped
75 g (3 oz) rice
2 tablespoons
  chopped parsley
2 tablespoons grated
  Parmesan cheese
salt and pepper

Shred the cabbage; chop the other vegetables and the bacon. Heat the oil in a large saucepan, add the bacon, onion, carrot, celery and garlic and fry gently, stirring frequently, for about 10 minutes.

Add the water, bring to the boil and add the cabbage, courgettes, tomatoes, sage or basil, and rice. Continue cooking gently for 20 minutes.

Stir in the parsley, cheese, and salt and pepper to taste.

Serve with extra Parmesan cheese and crusty bread.

Serves 6

NOTE: Small pasta may be used instead of rice.

Antipasti Misti

3 tomatoes, sliced
3 tablespoons olive
  oil
1 teaspoon chopped
  basil or spring
  onion tops
salt and pepper
1 fennel bulb
1 teaspoon lemon
  juice
1 clove garlic,
  crushed
6 slices Italian salami
6 slices garlic sausage
50 g (2 oz) black
  olives, drained
2 hard-boiled eggs,
  quartered
basil or parsley sprigs
  to garnish

Arrange the tomato at one end of a large oval dish and sprinkle with 1 tablespoon of the oil, the basil or spring onion tops, and salt and pepper to taste.

Trim the fennel, cut downwards into thin slices, then into strips. Mix the remaining oil with the lemon juice, garlic, and salt and pepper to taste. Add the fennel and toss well. Pile at the other end of the dish.

Arrange the salami and garlic sausage in the middle of the dish. Top with the olives and surround with the egg. Garnish with basil or parsley.

Serves 4

Antipasto alla Casalinga

2 green peppers
3 tablespoons olive
  oil
2 teaspoons wine
  vinegar
salt and pepper
4 tomatoes, sliced
few thinly sliced
  onion rings
1 × 198 g (7 oz)
  can tuna fish,
  drained and flaked
2 × 120 g (4¼ oz)
  cans sardines in
  oil, drained
TO SERVE:
2 tablespoons
  Maionese (see
  page 16)

Place the peppers under a preheated hot grill until the skin is charred and blistered, turning frequently. Cut in half and rinse under cold water to remove the skin and seeds. Drain well and slice finely. Mix with 2 tablespoons of the oil, the vinegar and a little salt. Leave in the refrigerator until required.

Season the tomato slices with salt and pepper to taste and sprinkle with the remaining oil. Arrange the pepper slices in a large serving dish and top with the tomatoes. Scatter the onion rings over the top.

Pile the tuna fish in the centre and surround with the sardines. Serve with the *Maionese*.
Serves 4

Carciofi alla Borghese

Dressed Artichoke Hearts

1 clove garlic, crushed
1 ½ tablespoons
  lemon juice
4 ½ tablespoons olive
  oil
salt and pepper
1 bay leaf
16 cooked fresh, or
  canned, artichoke
  hearts
1 tablespoon chopped
  parsley
	Beat together the garlic, lemon juice, oil, and salt and pepper to taste in a bowl. Add the bay leaf and artichoke hearts and stir gently. Cover and chill for about 2 hours, stirring occasionally. Discard the bay leaf.
	
	Divide the artichokes between individual dishes, spoon over the dressing and sprinkle with parsley.
	Serves 4

Caponata Palermitana

Sicilian Sweet-Sour Vegetables

3 large aubergines
salt and pepper
4 celery sticks
6 tablespoons olive
  oil
1 large onion,
  chopped
1 × 397 g (14 oz)
  can peeled
  tomatoes, drained
  and sieved
1 tablespoon tomato
  purée
2-3 tablespoons wine
  vinegar
2 tablespoons sugar
2 tablespoons capers
12 green olives,
  stoned
TO GARNISH:
1 tablespoon pine
  nuts or flaked
  almonds
2 hard-boiled eggs,
  quartered
	Cut the aubergines into 1 cm (½ inch) cubes. Sprinkle with salt, put into a colander, cover and leave for 1 hour. Rinse and dry with kitchen paper.
	
	Cook the celery in boiling water for 6 to 8 minutes. Drain and cut into 1 cm (½ inch) cubes.
	
	Heat 4 tablespoons of the oil in a large frying pan, add the aubergine and fry quickly, stirring frequently, for about 10 minutes until tender. Season to taste with salt and pepper.
	
	Heat the remaining oil in a large pan, add the onion and fry gently for 5 minutes. Add the celery and fry, stirring, for 5 minutes. Add the tomatoes, tomato purée and a little salt and pepper. Simmer gently until the celery and onion are tender, about 5 minutes.
	
	Add 2 tablespoons vinegar, the sugar, capers, olives and aubergine. Simmer for a few minutes, stirring. Adjust the seasoning and add extra vinegar if necessary. Cool, then cover and chill until required.
	
	Garnish with nuts and egg quarters to serve.
	Serves 4

Insalata di Funghi e Gamberi
Raw Mushroom and Prawn Salad

6 tablespoons olive oil
2 tablespoons lemon
  juice
pepper
1 clove garlic
350 g (12 oz) button
  mushrooms, thinly
  sliced
1/2 teaspoon salt
1 tablespoon chopped
  parsley
175 g (6 oz) peeled
  prawns

Beat the oil, lemon juice and a little pepper together in a mixing bowl. Add the garlic and mushrooms and stir gently. Cover and chill for at least 1 hour.

Just before serving, remove the garlic and stir in the salt and parsley. Transfer to a serving dish and top with prawns.

Serves 4

NOTE: Very fresh mushrooms and good olive oil are essential for this recipe.

Uova Sode Tonnata
Eggs with Tuna Mayonnaise

4 hard-boiled eggs
Maionese Tonnata
  (see page 17)
4 anchovy fillets
few capers
parsley sprigs to
  garnish

Cut the eggs in half lengthwise and arrange cut side down on individual dishes. Coat with *Maionese tonnata*.

Cut the anchovy fillets in half lengthwise and curl one strip on top of each egg half. Sprinkle with capers and garnish with parsley.
Serves 4

Prosciutto con Melone
Parma Ham with Melon

1 sweet ripe melon,
  chilled
4 slices Parma ham,
  or raw smoked
  ham

Cut the melon into quarters and remove the seeds. Drape the slices of ham over the melon. Serve with freshly ground black pepper.
Serves 4

Prosciutto e Fichi
Parma Ham with Figs

8 ripe purple figs
4 slices Parma ham,
  or raw smoked
  ham

Cut the figs almost through into quarters. Arrange the ham on individual plates and top with figs.
Serves 4

PASTA, RICE & PIZZAS

Risotto con Ragù
Risotto with Meat Sauce

1.2 litres (2 pints)
  chicken stock
  (approximately)
1 tablespoon oil
50 g (2 oz) butter
1 onion, finely
  chopped
350 g (12 oz) easy-
  cook Italian rice
25 g (1 oz) grated
  Parmesan cheese
salt and pepper
Salsa di Carne or
  Salsa di Fegatini
  (see pages 12-13)

Place the stock in a saucepan and bring to simmering point.

Heat the oil and half the butter in a heavy-based saucepan, add the onion and fry gently until soft and golden. Add the rice and cook, stirring, for 1 minute until translucent.

Add the stock a little at a time, adding more as each addition is absorbed and stirring frequently. Cook until the rice is just tender and the consistency creamy, about 10 minutes. Stir in the remaining butter, the cheese, and salt and pepper to taste.

Turn onto a warmed serving dish and pour the sauce into the centre. Serve with extra Parmesan cheese.
Serves 4

Risotto alla Paesana

Country-Style Risotto

3 tablespoons olive oil
1 onion, chopped
2 celery sticks, thinly sliced
125 g (4 oz) courgettes, thinly sliced
125 g (4 oz) shelled peas or broad beans
350 g (12 oz) easy-cook Italian rice
1.2 litres (2 pints) chicken stock (approximately)
25 g (1 oz) butter
125 g (4 oz) cooked ham, cut into strips
25-50 g (1-2 oz) grated Parmesan cheese
salt and pepper

Heat the oil in a heavy-based saucepan, add the onion and celery and fry gently for 3 minutes. Stir in the courgettes and peas or beans, cover and cook gently for 5 minutes. Add the rice and cook, stirring for 1 minute until translucent.

Add the stock, a little at a time, adding more as each addition is absorbed and stirring frequently. Cook until the rice is just tender and the consistency creamy, about 10 minutes. Stir in the butter, ham, cheese, and salt and pepper to taste.

Turn onto a warmed serving dish and serve immediately, with extra Parmesan cheese.

Serves 4

Pasta all' Uovo

Homemade Egg Pasta

250 g (8 oz) plain flour
2 large eggs
2 teaspoons oil
½ teaspoon salt
1 tablespoon water (approximately)

Sift the flour into a heap on a work surface and make a well in the centre. Put the eggs, oil and salt into the well and mix together with the fingers. Gradually work in the flour to form a crumbly dough. Knead to a firm but pliable dough, adding a few drops of water as necessary. Knead for 10 minutes, until smooth and elastic. Cover and leave to rise for 1 hour.

Roll out the dough on a lightly floured surface, first in one direction and then in the other, continuing until the pasta is paper thin. Shape and use as required (see below).
Makes 350 g (12 oz)

Pasta Verdi (Green Pasta)
Follow the above recipe, adding 50 g (2 oz) cooked sieved spinach (weighed after having been squeezed very dry) with the eggs. This pasta is softer than plain pasta and frequent flouring of the work surface may be necessary.

Shaping Pasta

Stuffed Pasta: The dough should be used immediately, without drying.

Flat and Ribbon Pasta: Dust the dough lightly with flour and leave to dry for 15 to 20 minutes, but do not allow to become brittle. Cut flat pasta into shapes as illustrated. Roll ribbon pasta into a loose Swiss roll and cut across into strips as illustrated opposite.

Cooking Pasta

Homemade Pasta: Put the pasta into a large pan containing 2.25 to 2.75 litres (4 to 5 pints) fast boiling water and 1½ tablespoons salt. Stir well, then boil steadily, uncovered, for 3 to 5 minutes until *al dente* – just tender but firm to the bite. Test frequently to avoid overcooking, as pasta continues to soften until you eat it. The moment it is done, tip the pasta into a colander, drain thoroughly and serve immediately.

Manufactured Pasta: As above, but follow the packet directions because cooking times are longer for manufactured pastas and vary considerably for different shapes and brands.

   Never break up long pasta such as spaghetti; simply bend it into the pan as it softens.

Quantities:

Allow 75 to 125 g (3 to 4 oz) pasta per person for a main course, 50 g (2 oz) for a starter.

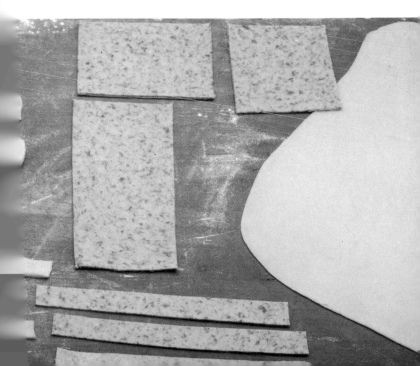

Tagliolini con Tonno

1 × 198 g (7 oz)
  can tuna fish
1 clove garlic, crushed
2 tablespoons
  chopped parsley
250 g (8 oz) ripe
  tomatoes, skinned
  and chopped
150 ml (¼ pint)
  chicken stock
salt and pepper
350 g (12 oz)
  tagliolini

Drain the oil from the tuna into a pan, add the garlic and heat gently for 2 minutes. Add the parsley and tomatoes and cook until the tomatoes begin to soften. Flake the tuna and add to the pan with the stock, and salt and pepper to taste. Simmer while cooking the pasta.

Cook the pasta in boiling salted water until *al dente*; drain well. Turn into a warmed serving dish. Add the sauce, toss and serve immediately.

Serves 4

Spaghetti alla Carbonara

350 g (12 oz)
  spaghetti
salt and pepper
175 g (6 oz) streaky
  bacon, derinded
  and chopped
3 eggs
3 tablespoons cream
40 g (1½ oz) grated
  Parmesan cheese
40 g (1½ oz) butter

Cook the spaghetti in boiling salted water until *al dente*; drain well.

Meanwhile, fry the bacon in its own fat until crisp. Drain well.

Beat the eggs with the cream, cheese, a little salt and plenty of pepper. Melt the butter in a large saucepan, add the egg mixture and stir until just beginning to thicken. Add the spaghetti and bacon, mix well and serve immediately.

Serves 4

Fettuccine al Gorgonzola

375 g (12 oz)
  fettuccini
salt and pepper
25 g (1 oz) butter
5 tablespoons milk
125 g (4 oz)
  Gorgonzola
  cheese, diced
120 ml (4 fl oz)
  double cream
25 g (1 oz) grated
  Parmesan cheese
1-2 tablespoons
  chopped basil
  (optional)

Cook the pasta in boiling salted water until *al dente*. Drain thoroughly.

Meanwhile, put the butter, milk and Gorgonzola cheese into a flameproof casserole. Place over a moderate heat and mash the cheese to a creamy sauce. Add the cream, and salt and pepper to taste and heat to simmering point.

Stir in the pasta, Parmesan cheese and basil if using. Toss until the pasta is coated, then serve immediately with extra Parmesan cheese.

Serves 4

Lasagne al Forno

175 g (6 oz) green
    lasagne
salt
450 ml (³/4 pint)
    Ragù Bolognese
    (see page 14)
600 ml (1 pint)
    Besciamella (see
    page 16)
40 g (1½ oz) grated
    Parmesan cheese

Cook the lasagne in boiling salted water until *al dente*. Drain, rinse in cold water, spread on clean tea-towels and pat dry.

Butter a 20 cm (8 inch) square ovenproof dish, at least 3.5 cm (1½ inches) deep. Spread a layer of *Ragù* on the bottom, cover with a layer of lasagne, then a layer of *Ragù* and finish with a thin layer of *Besciamella* and a sprinkling of cheese. Repeat these layers twice more, finishing with cheese.

Bake in a preheated moderately hot oven, 200°C (400°F), Gas Mark 6, for 20 to 25 minutes, until golden and bubbling. Serve immediately.
Serves 4 to 6

Tagliatelle alla Bolognese

350 g (12 oz)
    tagliatelle
salt
25 g (1 oz) butter
450 ml (³/4 pint) hot
    Ragù Bolognese
    (see page 14)
2 tablespoons grated
    Parmesan cheese

Cook the tagliatelle in boiling salted water until *al dente*. Drain thoroughly.

Melt the butter and pour into a deep serving dish, add 4 tablespoons of the *Ragù*, the pasta and Parmesan cheese. Toss lightly until the pasta is coated. Pile the remaining sauce on top and hand more cheese separately.
Serves 4

Cannelloni

12 flat pieces pasta,
   about 7.5 × 10 cm
   (3 × 4 inches)
salt and pepper
450 ml (³/₄ pint)
   Besciamella (see
   page 16)
300 ml (¹/₂ pint)
   Salsa di Pomodorì
   (see page 14)
3 tablespoons grated
   Parmesan cheese
25 g (1 oz) butter
FILLING:
2 tablespoons oil
1 onion, chopped
1 clove garlic, crushed
250 g (8 oz) finely
   minced beef
250 g (8 oz) frozen
   chopped spinach,
   cooked and
   squeezed dry
40 g (1¹/₂ oz) grated
   Parmesan cheese
1 egg yolk

Cook the pasta in boiling salted water until *al dente*, stirring occasionally. Drain, spread on a clean tea-towel and pat dry.

To prepare the filling, heat the oil in a saucepan, add the onion and garlic and fry gently until soft. Add the meat and cook, stirring, until well browned. Stir in the remaining ingredients. Bind the mixture with 2 tablespoons of the *Besciamella* and season well with salt and pepper.

Spread a rounded tablespoon of filling over each piece of pasta. Roll up loosely from the narrow side and place, join side down, in a buttered 20 cm (8 inch) square ovenproof dish.

Pour over the *Salsa di pomodori* and cover with the *Besciamella*. Sprinkle with cheese and dot with butter.

Bake in a moderately hot oven, 200°C (400°F), Gas Mark 6, for 15 to 20 minutes, until golden and bubbling.
Serves 4 to 6

Macaroni con Pomodori

Savoury Baked Macaroni

2 tablespoons oil
1 large onion, finely
　chopped
2 cloves garlic,
　crushed
1 small chilli pepper,
　seeded and finely
　chopped
4 rashers smoked
　streaky bacon,
　derinded and
　chopped
1 × 397 g (14 oz) can
　peeled tomatoes
1 teaspoon sugar
salt
250 g (8 oz)
　short-cut macaroni
50 g (2 oz) grated
　Provolone or other
　hard cheese

Heat the oil in a saucepan, add the
onion, garlic, chilli pepper and bacon
and fry gently for 10 minutes,
stirring occasionally. Add the
tomatoes with their juice, the sugar,
and salt to taste. Bring to the boil,
stirring, cover and simmer for
20 minutes.

Cook the macaroni in boiling
salted water until *al dente*; drain
thoroughly.

Arrange alternate layers of pasta,
sauce and cheese in an oiled
ovenproof dish, finishing with
cheese.

Serve immediately, or cover and
leave in a preheated cool oven, 140°C
(275°F), Gas Mark 1, for 20 to 30
minutes to allow the flavours to
blend.

Serves 3 to 4

Crespelle Ripiene
Spinach and Cheese Stuffed Pancakes

PANCAKE BATTER:
scant 125 g (4 oz) plain flour
¼ teaspoon salt
2 small eggs
1 tablespoon oil
150 ml (¼ pint) milk
6 tablespoons water

FILLING:
250 g (8 oz) frozen chopped spinach, cooked and squeezed dry
250 g (8 oz) Ricotta or curd cheese
25 g (1 oz) grated Parmesan cheese
1 egg, beaten
grated nutmeg
salt and pepper

TOPPING:
25 g (1 oz) butter
3 tablespoons grated Parmesan cheese
5 tablespoons chicken stock

Sift the flour and salt into a bowl. Make a well in the centre and add the eggs, oil and milk. Beat until smooth, then stir in the water. Cover and chill for 1 to 2 hours.

Lightly oil an 18 cm (7 inch) frying pan and place over moderate heat. When hot, pour in just enough batter to cover the base. When the pancake is set and the underside lightly browned, turn and briefly cook the other side. Repeat with the remaining batter, making 8 pancakes.

Mix the filling ingredients together, seasoning liberally with nutmeg, salt and pepper. Divide between the pancakes, roll up loosely and arrange in a buttered ovenproof dish. Dot with the butter, sprinkle with the Parmesan cheese and pour in the stock.

Bake in a preheated moderately hot oven, 200°C (400°F), Gas Mark 6, for about 20 minutes until golden. Serve immediately.
Serves 4

Pizza alla Casalinga
Home-Style Pizza

PIZZA DOUGH:
- 15 g (½ oz) fresh yeast
- 2 tablespoons warm water
- 250 g (8 oz) plain flour
- 1 teaspoon salt
- 2 tablespoons olive oil
- 3 tablespoons milk (approximately)

TOPPING:
- 3 tablespoons olive oil
- 500 g (1 lb) tomatoes, skinned, seeded and chopped
- 1 teaspoon dried oregano or basil
- salt and pepper
- 175 g (6 oz) Mozzarella cheese, sliced
- 4 tablespoons grated Parmesan cheese
- 6-8 black olives

Cream the yeast with the water. Sift the flour and salt into a bowl, make a well in the centre and pour in the yeast, oil and milk. Mix to a firm but pliable dough, adding a little more milk if necessary.

Turn onto a floured surface and knead vigorously for 5 minutes. Place in a clean basin, cover and leave to rise in a warm place until doubled in bulk.

Knead the dough lightly, then cut in half. Roll each piece into a 20 to 23 cm (8 to 9 inch) circle.

Place the circles on oiled baking sheets and brush with some of the oil. Cover with tomatoes and sprinkle with the herbs, and salt and pepper to taste. Add the cheese slices, then top with the Parmesan and olives.

Spoon over the remaining oil and leave to rise in a warm place for 30 minutes.

Bake in a preheated hot oven, 220°C (425°F), Gas Mark 7, for 25 to 30 minutes. Serve immediately.
Serves 4

Pizzette
Individual Pizzas

1 quantity risen Pizza
   dough (see opposite)
TOPPING:
3 tablespoons olive oil
500 g (1 lb) tomatoes,
   skinned, seeded
   and chopped
salt and pepper
TO FINISH:
125 g (4 oz)
   mushrooms, sliced
   and sautéed
2-3 garlic cloves,
   finely chopped
2-3 tablespoons
   grated Parmesan
   cheese

Divide the risen dough into
6 portions, shape into balls and roll
into 10 cm (4 inch) circles.

Brush with half of the oil, cover
with the tomatoes and season well.

Top with the mushrooms, garlic
and cheese. Sprinkle with the
remaining oil and leave to rise in a
warm place for about 15 minutes.

Bake in a preheated hot oven,
220°C (425°F), Gas Mark 7, for about
15 minutes. Serve immediately.

Serves 6

ALTERNATIVE FINISHES:
1. Chopped salami and olives.
2. Sliced peppers, diced Mozzarella
cheese and strips of anchovy fillet.

Sardenara
San Remo Pizza

1 quantity risen
   Pizza dough (see
   opposite)
TOPPING:
7 tablespoons olive
   oil
625 g (1¼ lb)
   onions, finely
   sliced
1-2 cloves garlic,
   crushed
1 × 397 g (14 oz)
   can peeled
   tomatoes, drained
1 teaspoon dried
   oregano
salt and pepper
1 × 49 g (1¾ oz)
   can anchovy
   fillets, cut in strips
20 black olives

To make the topping, heat 4
tablespoons of the oil in a saucepan,
add the onions and fry gently until
soft and golden. Add the garlic,
tomatoes, oregano, and a little salt
and pepper. Cook, uncovered, until
reduced and thickened. Check the
seasoning and leave to cool.

Turn the risen dough onto a
floured surface and knead lightly.
Cut in half, shape each into a ball and
place in well oiled 20 to 23 cm (8 to
9 inch) foil pie plates. Press out the
dough to cover the base of the plates
and reach 1 cm (½ inch) up the sides.
Brush with 1 tablespoon oil.

Spread the tomato mixture over
the dough and arrange the anchovy
strips and olives on top. Sprinkle
over the remaining oil.

Bake in a preheated hot oven,
220°C (425°F), Gas Mark 7, for 25 to
30 minutes. Serve immediately.

Serves 4 to 6

FISH

Spiedini di Scampi
Grilled Scampi

500 g (1 lb) frozen
   scampi, just
   thawed and dried
4 tablespoons olive
   oil
50 g (2 oz) dry
   white breadcrumbs
½ clove garlic,
   crushed
1 tablespoon finely
   chopped parsley
salt and pepper
lemon wedges
   to serve

Put the scampi in a bowl with the oil, breadcrumbs, garlic, parsley and salt and pepper to taste. Stir gently until thoroughly coated. Cover and leave to marinate for 30 minutes at room temperature.

Thread onto 4 kebab skewers, pushing them to the centre. Cook under a preheated very hot grill for 2 to 3 minutes on each side, depending on size, until the crumbs are crisp. Serve immediately, with lemon wedges.

Serves 4

Pesce alla Griglia
Marinated Grilled Fish

4 small mackerel,
   whiting, trout, or
   red or grey mullet,
   cleaned
salt and pepper
2 rosemary sprigs or
   bay leaves
4 tablespoons olive
   oil
1 ½ tablespoons
   lemon juice
1 small clove garlic,
   crushed (optional)
lemon wedges to
   garnish

Make 3 cuts across each side of the fish. Sprinkle with salt and pepper. Place the herbs in a shallow dish and lay the fish on top. Mix together the oil, lemon juice and garlic, if using, and pour over the fish. Cover and chill for 3 to 4 hours, turning several times.

Transfer the fish to the grill rack. Place about 10 cm (4 inches) under a preheated moderate grill and cook for 5 to 6 minutes on each side, until cooked through and golden.

Serve immediately, garnished with lemon wedges.

Serves 4

Sgombro en Cartoccio
Mackerel Parcels

4 × 250 g (8 oz)
  mackerel, cleaned
salt and pepper
3 tablespoons olive
  oil (approximately)
1 onion, finely
  chopped
2 celery sticks, finely
  chopped
1 tablespoon chopped
  parsley
1 clove garlic,
  crushed (optional)
½ teaspoon dried
  oregano or basil
juice of ½ lemon

Season the fish liberally with salt and pepper and brush with oil. Cut out heart-shaped pieces of foil 5 cm (2 inches) longer and wider than the fish; brush with oil.

Heat 2 tablespoons oil in a pan, add the onion and celery and fry gently for 10 minutes. Add the parsley, garlic, if using, herbs, lemon juice, and a little salt and pepper.

Lay a fish on each foil shape and top with the vegetable mixture. Fold over the foil, sealing the edges well, to enclose the fish. Place on a baking sheet and cook in a preheated moderately hot oven, 200°C (400°F), Gas Mark 6, for 25 to 30 minutes. Serve in the partially opened foil cases.
Serves 4

Pesce Gratinato al Forno

Golden Baked Fish

4 cod, hake or
    haddock steaks
salt and pepper
50 g (2 oz) dry
    white breadcrumbs
50 g (2 oz)
    Parmesan cheese,
    grated
MARINADE:
4 tablespoons olive
    oil
1 small clove garlic,
    crushed
2 mint or parsley
    sprigs, finely
    chopped
1/4 teaspoon dried
    oregano
TO GARNISH:
lemon quarters
parsley or mint sprigs

Combine the marinade ingredients in a shallow dish. Season the fish with salt and pepper and place in the marinade, turning to coat. Cover and leave in the refrigerator for 3 to 4 hours, turning once. Drain, reserving the marinade.

Mix together the breadcrumbs and cheese and use to coat the fish, pressing on firmly.

Strain the marinade into an ovenproof dish and add the fish. Spoon over enough marinade to moisten the coating. Cook in a preheated moderately hot oven, 190°C (375°F), Gas Mark 5, for 20 to 25 minutes. Garnish with lemon and herbs to serve.

Serves 4

Trotelle alla Savoia
Trout with Mushrooms

flour for coating
salt and pepper
4 trout, cleaned
2 tablespoons oil
65 g (2½ oz) butter
3 spring onions
    (green part only),
    chopped
350 g (12 oz) button
    mushrooms
1 tablespoon lemon
    juice
1 tablespoon chopped
    parsley
25 g (1 oz) dry
    white breadcrumbs
lemon wedges to
    garnish

Season the flour with salt and pepper and use to coat the trout.

Heat the oil and 25 g (1 oz) of the butter in a large frying pan, add the trout and fry gently for 6 minutes on each side until cooked and golden.

Meanwhile, melt the remaining butter in a pan, add the spring onion tops and mushrooms and fry for 3 minutes until the mushrooms begin to soften. Stir in the lemon juice, parsley and a little salt.

Arrange the trout and mushroom mixture on a warmed serving dish and keep hot.

Quickly fry the breadcrumbs in the fat remaining in the pan until crisp. Sprinkle over the fish and garnish with lemon wedges.
Serves 4

Sogliola all' Italiana
Sole or Plaice with Courgettes

4 tablespoons oil
1 onion, finely
 chopped
250 g (8 oz)
 tomatoes, skinned
 and chopped
1 teaspoon tomato
 purée
½ teaspoon dried
 basil
salt and pepper
4 small courgettes,
 thinly sliced
flour for coating
4 × 175 g (6 oz)
 sole or plaice fillets
25 g (1 oz) butter
2 tablespoons grated
 Parmesan cheese

Heat half the oil in a pan, add the onion and fry gently until soft. Add the tomatoes, tomato purée, basil and a little salt and pepper. Simmer, covered, for 5 minutes. Add the courgettes and simmer for 8 minutes, or until just tender.

Season the flour with salt and pepper and use to coat the fish. Heat the remaining oil with the butter in a large frying pan, add the fish and fry for 5 to 6 minutes on each side until cooked and golden.

Transfer to a shallow flameproof dish and top with the vegetable mixture. Sprinkle with cheese and place under a preheated moderate grill until lightly browned. Serve immediately.
Serves 4

Triglie alla Veneziana
Venetian-Style Red Mullet

5 tablespoons olive
  oil
1 large onion,
  chopped
300 ml (½ pint) dry
  white wine
1½ tablespoons wine
  vinegar
1-2 mint sprigs
2 cloves garlic,
  chopped
4 red mullet, cleaned
salt and pepper
flour for coating
TO GARNISH:
orange and lemon
  slices
mint sprigs

Heat 2 tablespoons of the oil in a pan, add the onion and fry gently until soft but not coloured. Add the wine and vinegar and boil briskly for 10 minutes or until reduced by half.

Meanwhile, put 2 or 3 mint leaves and a little garlic inside each fish. Season the flour well with salt and pepper and use to coat the fish.

Heat the remaining oil in a shallow frying pan, add the fish and fry gently until crisp, golden and cooked through, about 6 minutes on each side. Drain and arrange in a shallow dish. Pour over the hot sauce and leave to cool, basting occasionally.

Serve cold, garnished with orange and lemon slices and mint.
Serves 4

Maionese di Pesce
Italian Fish Mayonnaise

625 g (1¼ lb) white
  fish fillets (e.g. cod,
  haddock, rockfish)
salt and pepper
1 lemon
3-4 tablespoons olive
  oil
250 g (8 oz) frozen
  mixed vegetables
50 g (2 oz) peeled
  prawns
200 ml (⅓ pint)
  Maionese (see
  page 16)
TO GARNISH:
2 hard-boiled eggs,
  sliced
few stuffed olives,
  sliced
few drained capers
  (optional)

Put the fish in a pan and cover with cold water. Add 1 teaspoon salt and 2 lemon slices. Bring to simmering point and poach for 5 minutes or until cooked. Drain, skin and chop the fish. While still hot, flavour to taste with oil, salt, pepper and lemon juice. Cover and leave to cool.

Cook the vegetables as directed on the packet, drain and cool. Transfer to a serving dish and top with the fish and half the prawns. Pour over the *Maionese*, thinning with water if necessary. Garnish with the remaining prawns, the eggs and olives, and the capers if using.
Serves 4

MEAT

Petto di Vitello Ripieno
Stuffed Breast of Veal

1 kg (2 lb) piece
   boned breast of
   veal
25 g (1 oz) butter
STUFFING:
2 tablespoons oil
1 onion, chopped
250 g (8 oz) frozen
   chopped spinach,
   cooked and
   squeezed dry
250 g (8 oz) pork
   sausage meat
1 egg, beaten
3 tablespoons grated
   Parmesan cheese
salt and pepper

Fold the veal in half and sew two sides together to form a bag.

To make the stuffing, heat the oil in a saucepan, add the onion and fry until soft. Stir in the spinach, sausage meat, egg, cheese, and salt and pepper to taste. Stuff the veal with the mixture and sew up the open end.

Place in a casserole dish and dot with the butter. Cover and cook in a preheated moderate oven, 160°C (325°F), Gas Mark 3, for 2 hours, turning once.

Remove the thread and slice the veal. Serve hot, with the pan juices poured over, or cold with salad.
Serves 6

Scaloppine alla Parmigiana
Veal Escalopes with Ham and Cheese

500 g (1 lb) veal
    fillet, cut into
    4 slices
flour for coating
salt and pepper
1 tablespoon oil
40 g (1½ oz) butter
125 g (4 oz)
    Proscuitto or
    cooked ham,
    chopped
2 tablespoons
    chopped parsley
4 tablespoons grated
    Parmesan cheese
4 tablespoons chicken
    stock

Lay the veal slices flat between greaseproof paper and beat gently to flatten. Season the flour with salt and pepper and use to coat the veal.

Heat the oil and butter in a large frying pan, add the veal and fry for about 3 minutes on each side.

Mix the ham and parsley together and spread over the veal. Sprinkle with the cheese.

Stir the stock into the pan juices and spoon a little over each portion. Cover and cook gently for 5 minutes, or until the veal is tender and the cheese melting.

Transfer to a warmed serving dish and keep hot. Bring the pan juices to the boil and cook until reduced. Pour over the veal and serve immediately.
Serves 4

Involtini di Vitello alla Neapolitana
Stuffed Veal Rolls

500 g (1 lb) veal
  fillet, cut into
  8 thin slices
8 thin slices cooked
  ham or bacon
25 g (1 oz)
  breadcrumbs,
  soaked in milk and
  squeezed dry
3 tablespoons sultanas
25 g (1 oz) pine nuts
  or blanched
  slivered almonds
4 tablespoons grated
  Parmesan cheese
2 tablespoons
  chopped parsley
salt and pepper
1 tablespoon oil
25 g (1 oz) butter
150 ml (¼ pint) dry
  white wine
parsley sprigs to
  garnish

Lay the veal flat between greaseproof paper and beat gently to flatten. Cover each piece of veal with a slice of ham or bacon.

Mix together the breadcrumbs, sultanas, nuts, cheese and parsley, and season with salt and pepper to taste. Divide between the veal slices, roll up and secure each one with a cocktail stick.

Heat the oil and butter in a pan, add the veal rolls and fry until lightly browned. Pour in the wine, cover and cook very gently, turning once, for 20 to 25 minutes until tender.

Transfer the rolls to a warmed serving dish and keep hot. Bring the pan juices to the boil, stirring, and cook until well reduced. Spoon over the meat, garnish with parsley and serve immediately.

Serves 4

Vitello Tonnata
Veal with Tuna Fish Mayonnaise

1 kg (2 lb) piece
   boned and rolled
   shoulder of veal
1 carrot, halved
1 onion, halved
1 celery stick, sliced
1 bay leaf
4 peppercorns
salt
300 ml (½ pint)
   Maionese Tonnata
   (see page 17)
TO GARNISH:
strips of anchovy
   fillets
drained capers
few black olives
thin lemon slices

Put the meat into a saucepan just large enough to hold it. Add the carrot, onion, celery, bay leaf, peppercorns and 1 teaspoon salt. Add just enough water to cover and bring slowly to the boil. Skim the surface, cover and simmer for 1½ to 2 hours, until tender. Leave in the stock until cold.

Drain the meat and carve into neat slices. Lightly cover the base of a serving dish with half of the *Maionese tonnata* and arrange the meat on top. Spoon over the remaining dressing to cover the meat completely.

Cover the dish loosely with foil and leave in the refrigerator overnight.

Garnish with anchovies, capers, olives and lemon slices. Serve as an antipasto or main course.
Serves 4 to 6

51

Bistecca alla Pizzaiola
Steaks with Tomato and Garlic Sauce

4 rump, sirloin,
    forerib or flash-fry
    steaks
olive oil
salt and pepper
Salsa Pizzaiola (see
    page 15)
chopped herbs to
    garnish

Brush the steaks with oil and season with salt and pepper to taste.

Lightly oil the base of a frying pan and place over moderate heat. When hot, add the steaks and fry quickly for 2 minutes on each side.

Spread the steaks with the sauce, cover the pan and cook over low heat for 5 to 10 minutes, until tender.

Transfer to a warmed serving dish, garnish with herbs and serve immediately.

Serves 4

Stufatino alla Romana
Roman-Style Beef Stew

40 g (1½ oz) lard
1 small onion, finely
    chopped
25 g (1 oz) ham or
    bacon fat, finely
    chopped
1 celery stick, diced
1 clove garlic, sliced
750 g (1½ lb)
    stewing beef, cut
    into 2.5 cm
    (1 inch) cubes
¼ teaspoon dried
    marjoram
salt and pepper
200 ml (⅓ pint) full-
    bodied red wine
300-450 ml
    (½-¾ pint) beef
    stock
1 tablespoon tomato
    purée
TO SERVE:
1 large head celery,
    trimmed and cut
    into 5 cm (2 inch)
    lengths

Melt the lard in a heavy pan, add the onion and fry gently until transparent. Add the ham or bacon fat, celery and garlic and cook for 1 minute. Add the meat, marjoram, and salt and pepper to taste. Cook, stirring frequently, for 2 minutes.

Add the wine, bring to the boil and simmer until reduced by half. Add 300 ml (½ pint) of the stock and the tomato purée. Cover and cook very gently for 3 to 4 hours, until the meat is tender and the sauce is thick and rich. Stir occasionally and add the remaining stock a little at a time during cooking if the sauce reduces too quickly.

Meanwhile, cook the celery in boiling salted water for 15 to 20 minutes until tender. Drain and add to the stew just before serving, or serve separately.

Serves 4

Stracotto
Beef Braised in Wine

1 tablespoon oil
25 g (1 oz) butter
1 small onion,
  chopped
1 small carrot,
  chopped
1 celery stick,
  chopped
1.5 kg (3 lb) piece
  beef topside, boned
  aitchbone, top or
  middle rump
200 ml (⅓ pint)
  full-bodied red
  wine
200 ml (⅓ pint) beef
  stock
1 tablespoon tomato
  purée
1 thyme sprig
1 bay leaf
salt and pepper

Heat the oil and butter in a flameproof casserole, add the onion, carrot and celery and fry gently for 5 minutes, stirring occasionally.

Increase the heat, add the meat and cook, turning, until sealed. Add the wine, bring to the boil and simmer until well reduced.

Add the stock, tomato purée, herbs, and salt and pepper to taste. Bring to simmering point, cover and cook in a preheated cool oven, 150°C (300°F), Gas Mark 2, for 3 hours or until tender.

Slice the meat thickly, arrange on a warmed serving dish and keep hot.

Discard the herbs. If necessary, reduce the sauce to about 150 ml (¼ pint) by boiling uncovered, stirring frequently. Check the seasoning and spoon over the meat.
Serves 8

Fettine di Maiale alla Sorrentina

Sorrento-style Pork Slices

2 tablespoons oil
1 clove garlic, halved
4 boned pork loin
    chops
salt and pepper
1 large green pepper,
    cored, seeded and
    thinly sliced
1 × 227 g (8 oz) can
    peeled tomatoes
175 g (6 oz) button
    mushrooms, thinly
    sliced

Heat the oil and garlic in a large frying pan. When the garlic browns discard it.

Add the chops to the pan and brown lightly on each side. Season with salt and pepper to taste. Cover and cook very gently for 15 minutes. Remove from the pan and keep hot.

Add the pepper and tomatoes, with their juice, to the pan, stirring to break up the tomatoes. Cover and cook gently for 15 minutes.

Stir in the mushrooms and salt and pepper to taste. Cover and cook for 5 minutes.

Return the chops to the pan, baste with the sauce and simmer until hot through. Serve the chops with the sauce spooned over.

Serves 4

Maiale al Latte
Pork Cooked in Milk

1 tablespoon oil
25 g (1 oz) butter
1 clove garlic
1 rosemary sprig
1 kg (2 lb) piece
    boned and rolled
    loin of pork,
    derinded and
    secured with string
salt and pepper
600 ml (1 pint) milk

Heat the oil and butter with the garlic and rosemary in a flameproof casserole just large enough to hold the meat. Add the meat and fry, turning, until well browned all over. Season with salt and pepper to taste. Discard the garlic and rosemary.

Put the milk in a pan and bring to simmering point. Pour over the pork and cover, leaving the lid slightly tilted. Simmer for about 2 hours, turning occasionally, until the meat is tender and the milk reduced to about 150 ml (¼ pint).

Carve the meat into fairly thick slices, arrange on a warmed serving dish and keep hot. Skim off any surface fat from the milk, then stir, scraping the base of the pan to incorporate the meat residue. Reheat and spoon over the meat.
Serves 5 to 6

Abbacchio Brodettato

Spring Lamb in Lemon Sauce

750 g (1½ lb) boned
  shoulder or leg of
  lamb
25 g (1 oz) lard
50 g (2 oz) unsmoked
  gammon, chopped
1 onion, chopped
2 tablespoons flour
salt and pepper
4 tablespoons dry
  white wine or
  vermouth
300 ml (½ pint)
  light stock
2 egg yolks
2 tablespoons lemon
  juice
½ teaspoon finely
  grated lemon rind
1 teaspoon chopped
  marjoram
1 tablespoon chopped
  parsley

Cut the lamb into 2.5 cm (1 inch) cubes. Melt the lard in a heavy pan, add the gammon, lamb and onion and fry gently for 10 minutes, stirring frequently. Sprinkle in the flour and season to taste with salt and pepper. Cook, stirring, for 1 minute.

Add the wine or vermouth, bring to the boil and boil until reduced by half. Add the stock and bring back to the boil, stirring. Cover and simmer for 45 minutes, or until the lamb is tender. Skim off any surface fat.

Beat together the egg yolks, lemon juice and rind, and herbs. Add 3 tablespoons of the cooking liquor and blend well. Add to the pan and stir just until the sauce thickens; do not allow to boil. Check the seasoning and serve with ribbon noodles or new potatoes.
Serves 4

Abbacchio al Forno

Roast Lamb with Rosemary

1 × 1.5 kg (3 lb)
  leg of lamb
2-4 cloves garlic,
  sliced
3-4 rosemary sprigs
salt and pepper
1 tablespoon oil
150 ml (¼ pint) dry
  white wine or
  light stock
rosemary sprigs to
  garnish

Make small incisions in the lamb and insert a piece of garlic and a few rosemary leaves into each. Season with salt and pepper and place on a rack in a roasting pan. Spoon over the oil.

Cook in a preheated moderate oven, 180°C (350°F), Gas Mark 4, for about 2 hours. Transfer to a warmed serving dish and keep hot.

Skim the fat from the pan juices, add the wine or stock and bring to the boil, stirring, until thickened. Strain into a sauce boat and serve with the meat.
Serves 6

Agnello Piccante
Piquant Lamb Chops

8 best end of neck
    lamb chops
4 tablespoons olive
    oil
2 cloves garlic,
    chopped
2 teaspoons chopped
    marjoram
2 tablespoons
    chopped parsley
1 ½ tablespoons
    capers, drained
    and chopped
salt and pepper
1 tablespoon lemon
    juice
TO GARNISH:
sauté potatoes
lemon wedges

Lay the chops side by side in a dish, spoon the oil over them and sprinkle with the garlic. Cover and marinate for 2 hours, turning once.

Strain the marinade into a large frying pan, add the herbs and capers and heat gently. Add the chops and fry for 5 minutes on each side. Season with salt and pepper to taste, sprinkle with the lemon juice and cook, covered, over low heat for 5 minutes.

Pile the potatoes on a warmed serving dish and arrange the chops around the edge. Spoon some of the pan juices over the chops and garnish the dish with lemon wedges.
Serves 4

Animelle con Piselli
Sweetbreads with Peas

500 g (1 lb) lambs'
   sweetbreads
1 tablespoon vinegar
2 tablespoons oil
40 g (1½ oz) butter
2-3 sage sprigs,
   bruised
75 g (3 oz) smoked
   streaky bacon,
   derinded and diced
6 tablespoons
   Marsala
1 teaspoon lemon
   juice
salt and pepper
250 g (8 oz) shelled
   peas, cooked and
   drained

Soak the sweetbreads in cold water
for 1 hour. Drain, cover with fresh
water and add the vinegar. Bring to
the boil and simmer for 5 minutes.

Drain and peel any membranes
from the sweetbreads, then cut into
2.5 cm (1 inch) pieces.

Heat the oil and butter in a pan,
add the sage, bacon and sweetbreads
and cook over moderate heat, stirring
frequently, for 5 minutes. Add half
the Marsala and cook for about
5 minutes, until almost evaporated.

Add the remaining Marsala, the
lemon juice, and salt and pepper to
taste. Simmer until reduced and
thickened. Discard the sage, stir in
the peas and serve immediately, with
noodles.
Serves 4

Rognoncini Trifolati
Sautéed Kidneys

625 g (1¼ lb) lambs'
  or calves' kidneys
2 tablespoons vinegar
2 tablespoons oil
25 g (1 oz) butter
2 cloves garlic, finely
  chopped
2 tablespoons
  chopped parsley
1 tablespoon lemon
  juice
salt and pepper
small triangles of
  crisp fried bread to
  garnish

Cover the kidneys with cold water, add the vinegar and leave to stand for at least 30 minutes. Drain, cut out the core and thinly slice the kidneys.

Heat the oil and butter in a large frying pan. Add the garlic and kidneys and fry briskly, stirring constantly, for 2 minutes. Add the parsley, lemon juice, and salt and pepper to taste. Cook, stirring, for 1 to 2 minutes, until the kidneys are tender but juicy.

Serve immediately, garnished with fried bread triangles.
Serves 4

Polpette alla Siciliana
Meat Balls in Tomato Sauce

50 g (2 oz) bread,
  crusts removed,
  soaked in milk and
  squeezed dry
500 g (1 lb) minced
  veal or beef
2 cloves garlic,
  crushed
1 tablespoon chopped
  parsley
1 teaspoon finely
  grated lemon rind
25 g (1 oz) grated
  Parmesan cheese
grated nutmeg
salt and pepper
2 eggs, beaten
flour for coating
oil for shallow frying
300 ml (½ pint)
  Salsa di Pomodori
  (see page 14)

Put the bread, meat, garlic, parsley, lemon rind, cheese, and nutmeg, salt and pepper to taste into a bowl. Add the eggs and mix together lightly but thoroughly. Gently shape tablespoonfuls of the mixture into balls, 2.5 cm (1 inch) in diameter. Roll lightly in flour then place in the refrigerator until required.

Pour the oil into a large frying pan to a depth of 5 mm (¼ inch) and place over moderate heat. When hot, add the meat balls in batches, and fry for 3 to 4 minutes, turning, until brown on all sides. Lift out and drain on kitchen paper. Pour off the fat, leaving any residue in the pan.

Add the *Salsa di pomodori* to the pan, thinning to a pouring consistency with water if necessary. Return the meat balls to the pan, stir gently and simmer for 15 to 20 minutes until cooked through.
Serves 4

Pollo con Rosmarino
Chicken with Rosemary

4 chicken portions
salt and pepper
2 tablespoons oil
25 g (1 oz) butter
2-3 rosemary sprigs
2-3 cloves garlic
8 tablespoons dry
    white wine or
    chicken stock

Season the chicken with salt and pepper. Heat the oil, butter, rosemary and garlic in a large pan. Add the chicken and fry for 10 to 12 minutes until golden, turning once.

Add the wine or stock and bring to just below boiling point. Simmer, uncovered, for 20 to 30 minutes, until tender. Transfer the chicken to a warmed serving dish and keep hot.

Remove the rosemary and garlic and spoon off the surplus fat from the pan. Add 2 to 4 tablespoons water to the pan juices and bring to the boil, stirring to incorporate the sediment. Pour over the chicken to serve.

Serves 4

Petti di Pollo al Limone

Chicken Breasts with Lemon

4 boned chicken
  breasts
flour for coating
salt and pepper
1 tablespoon oil
65 g (2½ oz) butter
2 tablespoons lemon
  juice
3 tablespoons chicken
  stock
3 tablespoons
  chopped parsley
lemon slices to
  garnish

Cut each chicken breast horizontally into 2 slices. Season the flour with salt and pepper and use to coat the chicken pieces.

Heat the oil and 40 g (1½ oz) of the butter in a large frying pan, add the chicken and fry gently for 5 to 6 minutes on each side until tender. Transfer to a warmed serving dish and keep hot.

Add the lemon juice and stock to the pan juices, bring to the boil, stirring, and boil for 1 minute. Add the parsley and remaining butter and stir until blended.

Pour over the chicken and garnish with lemon slices to serve.

Serves 4

Pollo con Peperoni
Chicken with Peppers

flour for coating
salt and pepper
4 chicken portions
3 tablespoons oil
1 onion, thinly sliced
1 clove garlic, crushed
4 tablespoons dry
    white vermouth
1 teaspoon chopped
    marjoram
1 × 227 g (8 oz) can
    peeled tomatoes
1 teaspoon sugar
1 large green pepper,
    cored, seeded and
    sliced

Season the flour with salt and pepper and use to coat the chicken. Heat the oil in a large pan, add the onion and chicken and fry gently for 10 minutes until golden. Pour off surplus oil.

Add the garlic, vermouth and marjoram to the pan and simmer until the wine has almost completely evaporated. Add the tomatoes with their juice, the sugar and green pepper. Cover and simmer for 30 minutes or until the chicken is cooked. Lift the chicken onto a warmed serving dish and keep hot.

Boil the sauce briskly, uncovered, until reduced to a coating consistency. Check the seasoning and spoon over the chicken to serve.
Serves 4

Pollo con Salsa d'Uovo
Chicken in Egg and Lemon Sauce

4 chicken portions
salt and pepper
2 tablespoons oil
25 g (1 oz) butter
25 g (1 oz) plain
    flour
300 ml (½ pint)
    chicken stock
1 bay leaf
1 small marjoram
    sprig
2 egg yolks
1 tablespoon lemon
    juice
TO GARNISH:
1 tablespoon chopped
    parsley
lemon slices

Season the chicken with salt and pepper. Heat the oil and butter in a pan, add the chicken and fry gently for about 12 minutes until golden. Remove and set aside. Pour off all but 2 tablespoons of the fat.

Add the flour to the pan and cook, stirring, for 1 minute. Add the stock and bring to the boil, stirring. Return the chicken to the pan and add the bay leaf and marjoram. Cover and simmer for 30 minutes, until tender.

Transfer the chicken to a warmed serving dish. Discard the herbs. Blend the egg yolks and lemon juice with 3 tablespoons of the sauce. Add to the pan and heat gently, stirring, until thickened; do not boil. Adjust seasoning and pour over the chicken. Garnish with parsley and lemon.
Serves 4

Pollo in Porchetta
Chicken with Ham and Fennel

1 × 1.5 kg (3½ lb)
  oven-ready chicken
salt and pepper
175 g (6 oz) cooked
  ham, cut into thick
  strips
2 tablespoons
  chopped fennel
  stalks and leaves
2 cloves garlic,
  crushed
40 g (1½ oz) butter,
  softened
lemon juice
TO GARNISH:
Finocchio Toscano
  (see page 72)
fennel leaves

Season the chicken inside and out with salt and pepper. Mix together the ham, fennel and garlic and use to stuff the chicken. Place in a deep casserole dish and spread with the butter. Surround with the washed giblets, if retained.

Cover and cook in a preheated moderately hot oven, 200°C (400°F), Gas Mark 6, for 1 hour. Uncover and continue cooking, basting frequently, for 20 minutes until tender and golden brown. Transfer to a warmed serving dish and keep hot.

Discard the giblets if using. Season the juices with salt, pepper and lemon juice to taste and reheat. Garnish the chicken with *Finocchio alla toscano* and fennel leaves. Hand the sauce separately.
Serves 4

Pollo alla Diavolo
Tuscan Grilled Chicken

1 × 1.25 kg
  (2½ lb) oven-
  ready chicken
salt and pepper
MARINADE:
3 tablespoons olive
  oil
2 tablespoons lemon
  juice
2 cloves garlic,
  crushed
6 sage leaves

Halve the chicken along the breast
bone and cut out the back bone.
Flatten and skewer each wing and leg
together. Season liberally with salt
and pepper.

Mix the marinade ingredients
together in a shallow dish. Add the
chicken halves, turning to coat, cover
and chill for 4 hours, turning once.

Put the chicken, skin side down, in
a grill pan. Cook 13 to 15 cm
(5 to 6 inches) below a preheated
moderate grill for 12 minutes. Turn
and cook for a further 12 minutes or
until tender. Baste frequently with
the marinade while grilling.

Transfer to a warmed serving dish
and pour over the pan juices. Serve
with a green salad and crusty bread.
Serves 4

Filetti di Tacchino al Marsala

Turkey Breast with Marsala

500 g (1 lb) turkey
  breast
flour for coating
salt and pepper
1 tablespoon oil
65 g (2½ oz) butter
125 g (4 oz) button
  mushrooms, thinly
  sliced
1 teaspoon lemon
  juice
2 tablespoons grated
  Parmesan cheese
6 tablespoons
  Marsala
2 tablespoons chicken
  stock
cooked broccoli spears
  to garnish

Cut the turkey into 4 slices, 5 mm (¼ inch) thick. Season the flour with salt and pepper and use to coat the turkey. Heat the oil and 40 g (1½ oz) of the butter in a large frying pan, add the turkey and fry gently for 4 to 5 minutes on each side, until tender. Transfer to a warmed serving dish and keep hot.

Melt the remaining butter in the pan, add the mushrooms and fry briskly for 3 minutes. Add the lemon juice and a little salt and spread over the turkey slices. Sprinkle with the cheese.

Add the Marsala and stock to the pan and boil rapidly, stirring, until reduced by half. Spoon over the turkey. Garnish with broccoli to serve.

Serves 4

NOTE: Boned chicken breasts could be used instead of turkey.

Filetti di Tacchino alla Valdostano

Turkey Breast with Ham and Cheese

500 g (1 lb) boned turkey breast
flour for coating
salt and pepper
1 egg, beaten
2 tablespoons oil
25 g (1 oz) butter
4 slices cooked ham
125 g (5 oz) Bel Paese or Mozzarella cheese, thinly sliced
parsley sprigs to garnish

Cut the turkey into 4 slices, 5 mm (¼ inch) thick. Season the flour with salt and pepper and use to coat the turkey, then dip into the egg to coat. Heat the oil and butter in a large frying pan, add the turkey and fry for about 4 minutes on each side. Drain and transfer to a grill pan rack.

Cover each portion with a slice of ham and then with cheese. Place under a preheated hot grill for 1 minute, until the cheese is golden and bubbling. Serve immediately, garnished with parsley.

Serves 4

NOTE: Boned chicken breasts could be used instead of turkey.

Anitra alla Venezia
Venetian Roast Duck

1 × 2.25 kg (5 lb)
  duck
salt and pepper
2 teaspoons chopped
  sage
2 celery sticks,
  chopped
1 small onion,
  chopped
1 clove garlic, chopped
4 tablespoons
  Marsala
juice of 1 orange
150 ml (¼ pint)
  chicken stock
1 teaspoon lemon
  juice
TO GARNISH:
orange slices
parsley sprigs

Season the duck cavity liberally with salt and pepper and insert the sage, celery, onion and garlic. Prick the skin all over and place the duck breast down on a rack in a roasting pan.

Cook in a preheated moderate oven, 180°C (350°F), Gas Mark 4, for 1½ hours. Drain off the fat from the pan and turn the duck over. Heat the Marsala and orange juice and pour over the duck.

Continue roasting for 1 hour, or until tender, basting occasionally.

Transfer the duck to a warmed serving dish and keep hot. Skim the fat from the pan juices, add the stock and lemon juice and bring to the boil. Check the seasoning and strain into a sauceboat.

Garnish the duck with orange slices and parsley to serve.
Serves 4

Piccioncini en Tegame
Braised Wood Pigeons

4 wood pigeons
salt and pepper
2 tablespoons oil
25 g (1 oz) butter
1 onion, chopped
2 celery sticks,
  chopped
1 carrot, chopped
50 g (2 oz) streaky
  bacon, derinded
  and chopped
1 sprig each thyme,
  rosemary and sage
150 ml (¼ pint) dry
  white wine
300 ml (½ pint) hot
  chicken stock
350 g (12 oz)
  shelled peas

Season the pigeons inside and out with salt and pepper. Heat the oil and butter in a large flameproof casserole, add the onion, celery, carrot, bacon, and herbs tied together, and fry gently for 5 minutes. Add the pigeons and fry, turning until lightly browned.

Add the wine, bring to the boil and boil briskly for about 5 minutes. Add the stock, cover and cook gently for 1 to 1½ hours until the pigeons are almost tender.

Add the peas and cook for 15 to 20 minutes, until the pigeons and peas are tender. Discard the herbs, check the seasoning and serve immediately.
Serves 4

Fagiano alla Crema
Pheasant in Cream Sauce

1 young pheasant
salt and pepper
1 small onion, peeled
1 tablespoon oil
25 g (1 oz) butter
150 ml (¼ pint)
    double cream
2 teaspoons lemon
    juice
TO GARNISH:
cooked peas
cooked small carrots

Season the cavity of the pheasant liberally with salt and pepper and insert the onion. Heat the oil and butter in a flameproof casserole, add the pheasant and brown lightly all over.

Turn the bird breast side down and surround with the giblets, if using. Cover and cook in a preheated moderate oven, 180°C (350°F), Gas Mark 4, for 30 minutes. Turn the pheasant, pour over the cream and continue cooking, basting occasionally, for 20 to 30 minutes until tender.

Transfer the pheasant to a warmed serving dish and keep hot. Discard the giblets, if used. Add the lemon juice to the sauce and season with salt and pepper to taste. Cook, stirring, over moderate heat until smooth and thickened.

Pour over the pheasant and garnish with peas and carrots to serve.
Serves 3 to 4

Coniglio en Padella

Rabbit Stewed with Vegetables

1 aubergine, cut into
   2.5 cm (1 inch)
   cubes
salt and pepper
3 tablespoons oil
2 rashers streaky
   bacon, derinded
   and diced
1 celery stick,
   chopped
1 × 1 kg (2¼ lb)
   rabbit, jointed
4 large tomatoes,
   skinned and
   chopped
1 clove garlic, chopped
2 teaspoons each
   chopped marjoram
   and parsley
4 tablespoons
   Marsala
200 ml (⅓ pint)
   chicken stock
1 red or green
   pepper, cored,
   seeded and thinly
   sliced

Place the aubergine in a colander,
sprinkle with salt and leave for
1 hour. Drain, rinse and dry on
kitchen paper.

Meanwhile, heat the oil in a large
pan, add the bacon and celery and fry
gently for 2 minutes. Add the rabbit
pieces and fry until lightly browned.
Add the tomatoes, garlic, herbs and a
little salt and pepper and cook,
stirring, for 1 to 2 minutes.

Add the Marsala, bring to the boil
and simmer for about 5 minutes until
well reduced. Add the stock, cover
and simmer for 30 minutes.

Add the aubergine and pepper and
simmer for 30 minutes or until the
rabbit is tender. Transfer the rabbit
to a warmed serving dish and keep
hot.

If the sauce is too thin, boil briskly
for about 5 minutes until well
reduced. Check the seasoning and
spoon over the rabbit.

Serves 4

NOTE: Chicken portions could be
used instead of rabbit.

VEGETABLES & SALADS

Finocchio alla Toscano
Tuscan Baked Fennel

625 g (1¼ lb) fennel
   bulbs
salt and pepper
1 thick slice lemon
1 tablespoon oil
25 g (1 oz) butter
25 g (1 oz) grated
   Parmesan cheese
fennel leaves to
   garnish (optional)

Trim the fennel bulbs and remove any discoloured skin with a potato peeler. Cut vertically into 2 cm (¾ inch) thick pieces. Place in a pan with a pinch of salt, the lemon and oil and add sufficient boiling water to cover. Cook for 20 minutes or until just tender. Drain well.

Melt the butter in a gratin dish or shallow flameproof casserole, add the fennel and turn to coat. Season to taste with pepper and sprinkle with cheese.

Place under a preheated grill until lightly browned. Serve immediately, garnished with fennel leaves if liked.
Serves 4

Peperonata
Peppers with Tomatoes

4 tablespoons oil
250 g (8 oz) onions, chopped
2 cloves garlic, crushed
2 bay leaves
6 large green peppers, halved, cored and seeded
500 g (1 lb) tomatoes, skinned and chopped
salt and pepper

Heat the oil in a wide pan, add the onions, garlic and bay leaves and fry gently for 5 minutes, stirring occasionally.

Cut the peppers into 1 cm (½ inch) strips and add to the pan. Stir lightly, then cover and cook gently for 10 minutes.

Add the tomatoes and a little salt and pepper and cook uncovered, stirring frequently, until most of the liquid has evaporated and the mixture is fairly thick. Remove the bay leaves and check the seasoning.

Serve hot with grilled chicken, chops or steaks, or cold as an antipasto.

Serves 4

Sformata di Spinaci
Spinach Pudding

50 g (2 oz) butter
1 onion, grated
500 g (1 lb) chopped
   frozen spinach,
   thawed
25 g (1 oz) plain
   flour
200 ml (⅓ pint)
   milk
25 g (1 oz) grated
   Parmesan cheese
3 eggs, separated
salt and pepper
grated nutmeg
300 ml (½ pint)
   Salsa di Pomodori
   (see page 14)

Melt half the butter in a saucepan, add the onion and fry gently for 5 minutes. Stir in the spinach, cover and cook for 5 minutes. Uncover and cook, stirring, until the moisture has evaporated.

Melt the remaining butter in a clean pan, add the flour and cook, stirring, until browned. Add the milk and cook, stirring, for 2 minutes until thick and smooth. Remove from the heat and beat in the cheese, egg yolks, spinach, and salt, pepper and nutmeg to taste.

Whisk the egg whites until stiff and fold into the mixture. Turn into a well buttered 1.5 litre (2½ pint) pudding basin and cover with buttered foil. Place in a roasting pan half-filled with boiling water. Cook in a preheated moderate oven, 180°C (350°F), Gas Mark 4, for about 1 hour, until firm in the centre.

Leave for 5 minutes, then turn out onto a warmed serving dish and pour over the sauce to serve.
Serves 4

Fagioli alla Toscana
White Beans with Tomatoes

2 × 425 g (15 oz)
cans cannellini
beans, drained (see
below)
3 tablespoons olive
oil
2 cloves garlic,
crushed
1/2 teaspoon dried
sage
1 × 227 g (8 oz)
can peeled
tomatoes, drained
salt and pepper

Rinse the beans with cold water and drain.

Heat the oil, garlic and sage together gently in a saucepan for 1 to 2 minutes, then stir in the beans.

Press the tomatoes through a sieve into the pan. Add salt and pepper to taste and stir gently. Cover and simmer for 10 minutes.

Serve hot as a vegetable, or cold topped with tuna fish as an antipasto.
Serves 4
NOTE: If cannellini beans are unobtainable, cover 175 g (6 oz) dried haricot beans with boiling water and soak overnight. Next day, simmer gently for 1 1/2 to 2 hours until tender, drain and use as above.

Zucchini Ripieni
Cheese-Stuffed Courgettes

6 plump courgettes,
about 13 cm
(5 inches) long
salt and pepper
25 g (1 oz) white
bread, crusts
removed, soaked
in 2 tablespoons
milk
125 g (4 oz) Ricotta
or curd cheese
1 clove garlic, crushed
1/4 teaspoon dried
oregano
40 g (1 1/2 oz) grated
Parmesan cheese
1 egg yolk

Parboil the courgettes in boiling salted water for 5 minutes; drain. Cut in half lengthways and scoop out the centres; chop finely. Leave the shells on one side.

Squeeze the bread dry, reserving the liquid, and mix with the chopped courgette and remaining ingredients; add a little of the reserved milk if necessary to give a spreading consistency. Add salt and pepper to taste.

Fill the courgette shells with the mixture and arrange in a well oiled shallow baking dish.

Cook in a preheated moderately hot oven, 190°C (375°F), Gas Mark 5, for 35 to 40 minutes, until tender and golden.
Serves 4

Funghi Ripieni
Stuffed Mushrooms

12 large cup-shaped
  mushrooms
5-6 tablespoons olive
  oil
1 large onion,
  chopped
1 clove garlic, crushed
40 g (1½ oz) fresh
  breadcrumbs
50 g (2 oz) cooked
  ham or bacon,
  chopped
2 tablespoons
  chopped parsley
2 tablespoons grated
  Parmesan cheese
salt and pepper
parsley sprigs to
  garnish

Remove the stalks from the mushrooms and chop them finely. Heat 3 tablespoons of the oil in a pan, add the onion, garlic and chopped mushroom stalks and fry gently for 5 minutes. Add the breadcrumbs and fry until crisp, then stir in the ham or bacon, parsley, cheese, and salt and pepper to taste.

Arrange the mushroom caps, hollow side up, in a well oiled shallow ovenproof dish. Fill with the stuffing and sprinkle with a little oil.

Cover loosely with foil. Cook in a preheated moderately hot oven, 190°C (375°F), Gas Mark 5, for 25 minutes.

Serve hot, garnished with parsley, as a starter, or with chicken, meat or fish.
Serves 4

Gnocchi di Patate
Potato Gnocchi

175 g (6 oz) plain
  flour
1 egg, beaten
salt and pepper
grated nutmeg
500 g (1 lb)
  potatoes, boiled
  and mashed
TO SERVE:
25 g (1 oz) butter
25 g (1 oz) grated
  Parmesan cheese
Salsa di Fegatini or
  Salsa di Carne
  (see pages 12-13)

Combine the flour, egg, and salt, pepper and nutmeg to taste with the potato. Mix well to form a firm dough. With floured hands, shape pieces of the dough into long rolls, about 1 cm (½ inch) thick. Cut into 2 cm (¾ inch) lengths and curve by denting with a little finger.

Cook in batches, by dropping into a large pan of boiling salted water and simmering for 3 to 5 minutes until they rise to the surface. Lift out with a slotted spoon and drain. Place in a buttered shallow dish, dot with butter and sprinkle with Parmesan.

Place in a preheated moderately hot oven, 200°C (400°F), Gas Mark 6, for 7 to 10 minutes.

Divide between individual dishes and pour over the sauce.
Serves 4

Melanzane alla Parmigiana
Aubergine and Tomato Pie

750 g (1 ½ lb)
    aubergines
salt and pepper
flour for dusting
6 tablespoons olive
    oil (approximately)
300 ml (½ pint)
    Salsa di Pomodori
    (see page 14)
125 g (4 oz)
    Mozzarella or Bel
    Paese cheese,
    thinly sliced
3 tablespoons grated
    Parmesan cheese

Cut the aubergines lengthways into 5 mm (¼ inch) slices. Sprinkle with salt, place in a colander, cover and leave for 1 hour. Pat dry with kitchen paper, then dust lightly with flour.

Heat half the oil in a large frying pan, add half the aubergine slices and fry briskly until lightly browned on both sides. Remove with a slotted spoon and drain on kitchen paper. Repeat with the remaining oil and aubergine.

Fill an oiled 1.2 litre (2 pint) pie dish with alternate layers of *Salsa di pomodori*, aubergine, Mozzarella or Bel Paese and a sprinkling of pepper and Parmesan, finishing with Parmesan.

Bake in a preheated moderately hot oven, 200°C (400°F), Gas Mark 6, for 25 to 30 minutes until golden.
Serves 4

Insalata Mista
Italian Mixed Salad

Raw young spinach leaves are widely used for salads in Italy – when available, they make a nice change from lettuce. For a really crisp salad, after washing and thoroughly drying the lettuce or spinach, place in a polythene bag and leave in the refrigerator for a few hours.

1 crisp lettuce, or 125 g (4 oz) young spinach leaves
1/2 green pepper, cored, seeded and sliced
2 under-ripe tomatoes, sliced
1/2 small cucumber, sliced
6 radishes, sliced
DRESSING:
3 tablespoons olive oil .
1/2 tablespoon lemon juice
1 clove garlic, crushed
salt and pepper

Tear the lettuce or spinach leaves into pieces. Place in a salad bowl and top with the remaining vegetables.

Put the dressing ingredients in a screw-topped jar, adding salt and pepper to taste, and shake well.

Sprinkle the dressing over the salad and toss lightly together. Serve immediately.

Serves 4

Insalata di Finocchio
Fennel Salad

1 large fennel bulb
1/2 large cucumber, diced
4 radishes, sliced
2 oranges, divided into segments
DRESSING:
2 tablespoons olive oil
2 teaspoons lemon juice
1 clove garlic, crushed
2 teaspoons chopped mint
salt and pepper

Trim the stalks, base and coarse outer leaves from the fennel, cut downwards into thin slices, then into strips.

Put in a salad bowl with the cucumber, radishes and orange segments.

Put the dressing ingredients in a screw-topped jar, adding salt and pepper to taste, and shake well. Sprinkle over the vegetables and toss lightly. Serve immediately.

Serves 4

Insalata di Rinforza
Cauliflower Salad

1 cauliflower, broken
　　into florets
salt and pepper
5 tablespoons olive
　　oil
1½ tablespoons wine
　　vinegar
1 tablespoon capers,
　　drained
1 tablespoon chopped
　　parsley
few black olives
1 × 49 g (1¾ oz)
　　can anchovy
　　fillets, drained and
　　sliced

Cook the cauliflower in boiling
salted water until cooked but firm,
about 5 to 6 minutes. Drain and rinse
under running cold water.

Mix the oil, vinegar and a little salt
and pepper together in a salad bowl.
Add the cauliflower and toss gently.
Sprinkle with the capers, parsley and
olives. Arrange the anchovy fillets in
a lattice pattern on top. Serve
immediately.
Serves 4

Insalata di Riso
Rice Salad

250 g (8 oz)
   easy-cook Italian
   rice
2 teaspoons salt
600 ml (1 pint) cold
   water
4 tablespoons olive
   oil
1 tablespoon wine
   vinegar
2 spring onions,
   finely chopped
1 small green pepper,
   cored, seeded and
   thinly sliced
salt and pepper
¼ cucumber, diced
2 tablespoons
   chopped parsley
crisp lettuce leaves

Put the rice, salt and water in a pan and bring to the boil. Stir, cover tightly and simmer gently for 15 minutes. Uncover and cook for 1 to 2 minutes until the liquid is completely absorbed.

Combine the oil, vinegar, spring onions, green pepper, and plenty of salt and pepper in a bowl. Add the hot rice and toss together thoroughly. Cover and leave until cold.

Just before serving, stir in the cucumber and parsley. Line a shallow bowl with lettuce, pile the rice salad in the centre and serve immediately.
Serves 4 to 6

DESSERTS

Melone con Fragoline
Melon with Strawberries

1 melon
icing sugar for
   dusting
350 g (12 oz) small
   strawberries,
   hulled
2 tablespoons
   Cointreau or
   Grand Marnier
juice of ½ lemon

Cut a 'lid' off the top of the melon
and reserve. Scoop out the flesh with
a melon baller, discarding the seeds;
alternatively, cut into small cubes.
Reserve the shell. Sprinkle the melon
flesh with a little icing sugar, cover
and chill until required. Sprinkle the
strawberries with the liqueur, lemon
juice and icing sugar to taste, cover
and chill until required.

   Just before serving, mix the melon
and strawberries together, pile into
the melon shell and cover with the
'lid'. Serve on a bed of crushed ice
decorated with flowers and mint, if
liked.
Serves 4

Pesche alla Piemontese
Almond Stuffed Peaches

4 large firm peaches,
 halved and stoned
75 g (3 oz)
 macaroons,
 crushed
50 g (2 oz) caster
 sugar
40 g (1½ oz) butter,
 softened
1 egg yolk
½ teaspoon finely
 grated lemon rind
flaked almonds to
 decorate (optional)

Scoop a little flesh from the centre of each peach half and put in a basin. Add the macaroon crumbs, sugar, 25 g (1 oz) of the butter, the egg yolk and lemon rind and beat until smooth.

Divide between the peaches, shaping the stuffing into a mound. Top with flaked almonds if liked, and dot with the remaining butter. Arrange in a buttered ovenproof dish.

Bake in a preheated moderate oven, 180°C (350°F), Gas Mark 4, for 25 to 35 minutes. Serve warm or cold with pouring cream.
Serves 4

Zabaglione

4 egg yolks
50 g (2 oz) caster
  sugar
8 tablespoons
  Marsala
sponge fingers to
  serve

Put the egg yolks and sugar in a basin and whisk until pale and foamy. Place the basin over a pan of almost boiling water, making sure the bottom of the basin does not touch the water; whisk in the Marsala. Continue whisking until the mixture expands to form a dense foamy mass that just holds its shape. Spoon into wine glasses and serve immediately, with sponge fingers.
Serves 4

Cassata alla Siciliana

3 medium eggs
75 g (3 oz) caster
  sugar
½ teaspoon finely
  grated lemon rind
½ teaspoon vanilla
  essence
scant 75 g (3 oz)
  plain flour, sifted
FILLING AND ICING:
500 g (1 lb) Ricotta
  or curd cheese
125 g (4 oz) caster
  sugar
4 tablespoons
  Maraschino or
  Cointreau
50 g (2 oz) plain
  chocolate, finely
  chopped
50 g (2 oz) chopped
  mixed peel
1 tablespoon chopped
  pistachio nuts or
  almonds
TO DECORATE:
glacé cherries
orange and lemon
  slices
grated chocolate

Beat the eggs, sugar, lemon rind and vanilla together, using an electric or rotary whisk, until thick enough to hold its shape. Fold in the flour.

Turn into a lined and greased 1.2 litre (2 pint) loaf tin. Cook in a preheated moderately hot oven, 190°C (375°F), Gas Mark 5, for 20 to 30 minutes, until firm. Turn onto a wire rack to cool.

Beat the cheese and sugar together until smooth and light. Add 2 tablespoons of the liqueur. Divide the mixture in half. Place one portion in the refrigerator for the icing. Mix the chocolate, peel and nuts into the other portion for the filling.

Cut the sponge horizontally into 3 layers. Place the bottom layer on plate, sprinkle with 1 tablespoon liqueur and spread with half the filling. Cover with the middle layer, then the remaining liqueur and filling. Cover with the top sponge layer, press together and chill.

About an hour before serving, spread the icing evenly over the top and sides of the gâteau. Decorate with candied fruit and chocolate.
Serves 6

Crostata Dolce di Ricotta
Italian Curd Tart

FLAN PASTRY:
*250 g (8 oz) plain
   flour, sifted
75 g (3 oz) caster
   sugar
125 g (4 oz) butter,
   softened
1 teaspoon finely
   grated lemon rind
2 egg yolks*
CURD FILLING:
*350 g (12 oz)
   Ricotta or curd
   cheese, sieved
75 g (3 oz) caster
   sugar
3 eggs, beaten
1 teaspoon each
   grated lemon and
   orange rind
75 g (3 oz) candied
   peel, chopped
50 g (2 oz) blanched
   almonds, chopped*
TO DECORATE:
icing sugar

Mix together the flour and sugar in a bowl, make a well in the centre and add the butter, lemon rind and egg yolks. Gradually draw the flour into the centre, using the fingertips, and work the ingredients to a firm, smooth dough. Cover and chill for 1 hour.

Meanwhile, prepare the filling. Mix the cheese and sugar together in a basin. Gradually beat in the eggs, then add the remaining ingredients. Mix well.

Roll out the pastry and use to line an 18 to 20 cm (7 to 8 inch) flan ring standing on a baking sheet. Spread the filling evenly in the flan case.

Bake in a preheated moderate oven, 180°C (350°F), Gas Mark 4, for 45 to 50 minutes. Cool slightly, then transfer to a wire rack and leave until cold. Sprinkle with icing sugar to serve.

Serves 6 to 8

NOTE: If preferred, decorate the tart with a lattice pattern of pastry strips, before baking.

Nocciollette

Hazelnut Cookies

75 g (3 oz)
   hazelnuts
125 g (4 oz) butter
40 g (1½ oz) icing
   sugar
1½ tablespoons
   honey
125 g (4 oz) plain
   flour
icing sugar for
   dusting

Spread the nuts on a baking sheet and place under a preheated moderate grill until the skins split, shaking frequently. Turn into a rough towel and rub off the loose skins. Grind coarsely.

Cream the butter, sugar and honey together until fluffy. Add the flour and nuts and mix to a dough.

With lightly floured hands, shape teaspoonfuls of the mixture into ovals and place about 5 cm (2 inches) apart on lightly oiled baking sheets.

Bake in a preheated moderate oven, 180°C (350°F), Gas Mark 4, for about 15 minutes, until firm. Cool slightly, then roll in icing sugar. Transfer to a wire rack and leave until cold. Store in an airtight tin.
Makes about 24

Pastini di Mandorle

Almond and Apricot Cookies

125 g (4 oz) butter,
  softened
200 g (7 oz) caster
  sugar
1 medium egg,
  beaten
4 drops almond
  essence
250 g (8 oz) plain
  flour
1 teaspoon baking
  powder
1 tablespoon milk
  (approximately)
50 g (2 oz) blanched
  almonds, finely
  chopped
2 tablespoons apricot
  jam

Cream the butter and sugar together until light and fluffy, then beat in the egg and almond essence. Sift the flour and baking powder together and stir into the mixture with enough milk to form a smooth paste.

Roll teaspoonfuls of the mixture into balls. Roll in chopped almonds and place well apart on a greased baking sheet. Make a deep dent in the centre of each and fill with jam.

Bake in a preheated moderately hot oven, 200°C (400°F), Gas Mark 6, for 12 to 15 minutes, until golden. Leave for 5 minutes then transfer to a wire rack and leave until cold. Store in an airtight tin.
Makes about 36

Gelato alla Nocciola

Hazelnut Ice Cream

100 g (3½ oz)
  hazelnuts, toasted
  and skinned (see
  Nocciolette,
  page 87)
300 ml (½ pint)
  milk
4 egg yolks
75 g (3 oz) caster
  sugar
3 drops vanilla
  essence
175 ml (6 fl oz)
  whipping cream,
  whipped

Reserve a few nuts for decoration if liked; grind the remainder coarsely.

Place the milk in a pan and bring almost to the boil. Cream together the egg yolks, sugar and vanilla essence in a bowl until pale, then gradually stir in the milk. Stir in the ground nuts.

Pour into a clean saucepan and heat gently, stirring, until the mixture is thick enough to coat the back of the spoon; do not allow to boil. Cover and leave until cold, stirring occasionally.

Fold the cream into the custard. Turn into individual freezerproof containers, cover and freeze until firm.

Transfer to the refrigerator 1 hour before serving to soften. Decorate with nuts if reserved, before serving.
Serves 4 to 5

Gelato di Fragole
Strawberry Ice Cream

250 g (8 oz) ripe
    strawberries
juice of ½ orange
2 teaspoons lemon
    juice
50-75 g (2-3 oz)
    icing sugar
200 ml (⅓ pint)
    whipping cream
few strawberries,
    halved, to decorate

Purée the strawberries in an electric blender or rub through a sieve, then strain. Stir in the orange and lemon juices and sweeten to taste with icing sugar. Whip the cream until thick but not stiff. Gently fold in the strawberry mixture. Turn into a freezerproof container, cover and freeze until firm.

Transfer to the refrigerator 1 hour before serving to soften. Spoon into individual glass dishes and decorate with strawberries to serve.

Serves 3 to 4

Granita di Arancia
Orange Water Ice

250 g (8 oz)
  granulated sugar
600 ml (1 pint)
  water
300 ml (½ pint)
  unsweetened
  orange juice
2 tablespoons lemon
  juice
1 teaspoon finely
  grated orange rind

Place the sugar and water in a pan over moderate heat and stir until dissolved. Bring to the boil and boil for 5 minutes. Cool to room temperature, then stir in the fruit juices and orange rind.

Pour into a shallow freezerproof tray. Freeze to a snowy, granular texture, stirring every 30 minutes.

Spoon into 4 tall glasses and serve immediately, with a straw or spoon.

Serves 4

NOTE: If the ice freezes solid, transfer to the refrigerator to soften until it can be mashed with a fork.

Granita di Limone

Make as above, replacing the orange and lemon juice and orange rind with 300 ml (½ pint) fresh lemon juice.

Gelato Agli Amaretti

Amaretti Ice Cream

100 g (3½ oz)
   amaretti or
   macaroons
3 tablespoons
   Marsala or
   medium sherry
   (approximately)
450 ml (¾ pint)
   vanilla ice cream
   (see below)
TO DECORATE:
whipped cream
   (optional)
ratafia biscuits

Grind the *amaretti* or macaroons in an electric blender or crush with a rolling pin. Mix to a soft paste with the Marsala or sherry.

Spread two thirds of the ice cream over the base and two-thirds up the sides of a 600 ml (1 pint) basin. Spread the macaroon mixture in the centre and cover with the remaining ice cream, smoothing the top. Cover with foil and freeze until required.

Turn the ice cream out onto a serving dish and place in the refrigerator 30 minutes before serving to soften. Decorate with whipped cream, if using, and ratafia biscuits to serve.

Serves 4

NOTE: Avoid soft ice cream otherwise the bombe will not hold its shape.

Panforte di Siena

This flat 'cake' with a nougat-like texture, rich with candied peel, toasted nuts and spices, is a particular speciality of the town of Siena. Although it can be served as a dessert to round off a light meal, Italians would be more likely to serve it with coffee in the morning or mid-afternoon.

75 g (3 oz) hazelnuts

75 g (3 oz) blanched almonds, coarsely chopped

175 g (6 oz) candied peel, finely chopped

25 g (1 oz) cocoa powder

50 g (2 oz) plain flour, sifted

½ teaspoon ground cinnamon

¼ teaspoon ground mixed spice

125 g (4 oz) caster sugar

125 g (4 oz) clear honey

TO FINISH:

2 tablespoons icing sugar

1 teaspoon ground cinnamon

Spread the nuts on a baking sheet and place under a preheated moderate grill until the skins split, shaking frequently. Turn into a rough towel and rub off the loose skins. Grind the hazelnuts coarsely.

Place the hazelnuts, almonds, candied peel, cocoa powder, flour and spices in a mixing bowl and stir well.

Put the sugar and honey in a pan and heat gently until the sugar has melted. Boil gently until a little of the mixture forms a soft ball when dropped into a cup of cold water. Remove from the heat and stir in the dry ingredients.

Press into a lined and greased 20 cm (8 inch) loose-bottomed flan tin so that the mixture is no more than 1 cm (¼ inch) thick. Bake in a preheated cool oven 150°C (300°F), Gas Mark 2, for 30 to 35 minutes.

Remove from the flan tin and allow to cool. Peel off the lining paper and transfer to a serving plate. Mix the icing sugar with the cinnamon and sift over the 'cake'. Serve cut into wedges.

Serves 8 to 10

INDEX

Acknowledgments

Photography by Roger Phillips
Food prepared by Jackie Burrow and Caroline Ellwood
Designed by Astrid Publishing Consultants Ltd.
The publishers would also like to thank The Pasta
Information Bureau for supplying pasta for photography.